GOOD!S

SHAKING THE CANADIAN
ADVERTISING TREE

JERRY GOODIS
with
Gene O'Keefe

Fitzhenry & Whiteside

DOUGLAS COLLEGE LIBRARY

GOOD!S

Copyright © 1991 Fitzhenry & Whiteside

No part of this publication may be reproduced in any form without permission in writing from the publisher.

Fitzhenry & Whiteside Ltd. 195 Allstate Parkway Markham, Ontario L3R 4T8

Editor: Fraser Sutherland
Designer: McCalla Design Associates
Typesetter: Jay Tee Graphics Ltd.

Canadian Cataloguing in Publication Data

Goodis, Jerry
   Jerry Good!s :
Shaking the Canadian Advertising Tree

ISBN 1-55041-013-X

1. Goodis, Jerry. 2. Advertising – Canada.
3. Advertising – Canada – Biography. I. Title.
II. Title: Jerry Goodis : True Confessions While Shaking the Canadian Advertising Tree

HF5810.G6A3 1991   659.1'092   C91-093545-9

Printed and bound by R.R. Donnelly & Sons, USA

CONTENTS

For
Joyce Seidel-Goodis
and
Dr. Leslie Ruth Goodis
David Seth Goodis
Noah Lee Goodis

All of whom practise excellence
instead of merely searching for it.

ACKNOWLEDGEMENTS

His secretary appeared in the lavish, rather overbearing reception area of the legal firm Goodman & Goodman's Toronto office and delivered the ritualistic "he'll see you now".

After a mile-long hike through the maze, I walked into Michael Levine's office. He was, as always, speaking on the telephone, this time exhorting Charles (Bronfman, I think) to "stop worrying so much", looked up, waved me down into the chair before his indescribably pink desk (pink from the dozens of pink phone message slips beautifully stacked in neat piles edge to edge on his desk). He said to Charles "see you next week", put the phone down, looked up at me and said: "Jerry Goodis, my favourite phoenix. . . ."

Michael is Canada's pre-eminent lawyer to the Canadian cultural community. Actors, actresses, writers, film producers, authors, announcers, directors, artists . . . the cream of Canada's healthy crop are protected by Michael. He's one of three lawyers who act for me in various business ventures.

And I love the man . . . for his intellect, his humour, his charm, his brilliance, his patience. He is the lawyer to whom I entrusted my partnership agreement and subsequent dissolution with friend Avie Bennett. [Avie is responsible for bringing me temporarily back into the crazy world of Canadian advertising in 1988.] Avie believes in me, he put up an enormous amount of cash, and publicly proclaimed that Jerry Goodis deserves a second shot at waking up the merger-ridden industry . . . and put his money where his mouth was. I shall never forget that brotherly gesture. As it turns out, it had a happy ending; Goodis & Sharabura merged with Lowe Case, everybody (but me) kept their jobs while the indomitable David Hughes and I left the merged entity and started our Venture Marketing practice, Goodis & Hughes, Inc.

I laboured over this book with friend Gene O'Keefe for almost a year. I did some research; dear wife, Joyce, did some research; Gene did some. But mostly the research was executed by Adina Trowhill who deserves a thank you and much more money than we paid her. Randy Scotland, the senior writer at *Marketing* Magazine was so helpful in supplying historical background to Gene O'Keefe and me. Wunderman Worldwide, particularly Heather Albrecht, were cheerfully co-operative in checking the facts in those chapters which have to do with direct marketing. I am, after all, a competitor of theirs, but they were gracious enough to lend an important hand in the crafting of this book.

As for Gene O'Keefe, if this were a war he should be awarded the Victoria Cross. He had to endure hours of taping, days and days of rambling, unconnected thoughts, unremembered incidents, and he had to make sense out of the whole thing. Gene, a true professional, was the only writer I could think of who could survive the ordeal.

Lawyer John Pollock, a lifetime friend and my major legal fount of advice and support (and protection from the snakes and rabid wolves in the advertising jungle) has, however, been the pillar of support in my career thus far. John has put a spring in my gait in the autumn of that career. How? With a continuous and single-minded reassurance about my abilities (grossly overstated by John Robert Colombo in the Foreword to this book, God bless him) and wily counsel in a couple of sticky situations I managed to get myself into, which John got me out of. John throws people with his happy, upbeat countenance. He is the most creative, innovative lawyer I have ever known.

John H. Pollock, Q.C.

Through good times and bad, John calls me every single day. Every single day — just to keep my spirits up, but mostly because he cares. He and his dear wife, Molly, are friends that one in ten million people have. His collection of Judaica, his definitive collection of Holocaust literature (which he is about to endow to a major Canadian university), his collection of Canadian art and artifacts (he represents at the time of the writing of this "final word", A.J. Casson, the lone surviving member of the Group of Seven), reveal John as an uncommon human being.

If there is anything at all wrong with his character it is that he is a hapless Progressive Conservative. And that's because, before and during the Second World War, the anti-Semitic Liberal government turned away the ship *Exodus* and thousands of other Jews fleeing from Hitler's gas chambers. John has never forgiven them, even though those old anti-Semitic bastards were turfed out by Keith Davey and Lester B. Pearson in the fifties. John's principles are unquestioned, but the son of a gun is just as Liberal as I am, if the truth be known.

And Keith Davey? An amazing parallel exists in character and personality between the Senator and Johnny Pollock. Keith, whom I regard as one of my closest friends, has shared the trenches with me, too. Keith introduced me to politics, to Mr. Pearson, to Pierre Trudeau and the Liberal Party with

Senator Keith Davey

whom I am still deeply involved. As an adviser, mentor, and friend, Keith has, however, no parallel. Like John Pollock, he has been next to me on my drive down through the valleys and up to the peaks, never once, *not once*, giving up on me in spite of my stubbornness, my arrogance, and, ofttimes, my sheer stupidity. Keith and Dorothy have been my port through the storms of my life.

While Senator Davey is recognized, even by Tories, as this continent's shrewdest political strategist, he has a sense of humour at all times — except during election campaigns. If he is a political animal, Keith is a political animal in heat during an election. He was impossible and humourless in elections, even when we Liberals were certain to sweep the country. At all other times, he's warm, funny, brilliant. When I married Joyce, in the home of another very dear friend, Dr. Stan Greben, Keith, who was the appointed Master of Ceremonies, took me aside to warn me that he was going to begin his remarks with the observation that "I speak at all of Jerry's weddings." I was aghast — and Dorothy and I threatened the most dire of consequences if he came within twenty miles of that opening. He didn't.

David Harrison, the king of Canada's strategic media-buying community and the industry's most incisive thinker, has been mentor, friend, and supporter ever since we worked together at MacLaren. Charming and elegant, his advice and direction to me is always fresh, decisive, and uncannily and invariably similar to mutual friend Keith Davey's insights. To have David Harrison beside you in the trenches is more effective than being armed with an Uzi machine gun and a steel helmet. Cool under fire with a built-in business sense — that's what got David and Harrison, Young, Pesonen and Newell to the top.

Dr. Stan Greben, like no other friend or professional, has helped me understand why I do what I do, respond like I respond, feel like I feel. He's there for me, too, on stormy and on calm days. He has intellect and he has empathy and he is a giver and a terrific human being. I am a lucky guy to have such mentors. They have lifted my self-esteem whenever unscrupulous opportunists have played on the worst in me for their own gain; on my pride, my conceit, my arrogance.

Dr. Stan Greben

One last word about the most important partner, counsellor, and support I have ever had. My darling wife, Joyce.

Brilliant, beautiful, cunning. Tough and principled. It

never mattered how stubborn, bull-headed, and naïve I was about people, situations, opportunities, or disasters, Joyce Seidel-Goodis was, is, and always will be patient, cool, understanding, and loving.

She believes in me.

I didn't want to write this book.

She insisted.

I trust everybody . . . my Achilles heel.

She blows the whistle when I'm taken in yet again.

I gave up, a couple of times. She picked me up, brushed me off, applied a Band-Aid to the knee and started me over again. Her incredible insight into people, her built-in fraud detector, and her reservoir of common sense is a wonder to behold and a pleasure to experience, especially in the middle of a crisis.

You don't cross Joyce. She is, to a fault, protective of her dignity and mine. She is a great balance to my up-and-down personality. I love her, and Leslie Ruth, David Seth, and Noah Lee (my children) more than I can commit to paper.

Yes, there are brother Albert Soren, Drs. May and Jerry Cohen, Jack Scheckowitz, Ralph Lean, Arthur Jacques, George Mara, John Bitove, Douglas Fowles, Pierre Trudeau, Alec Peck, Otto Lang, Brian Perlman, Michael Doherty, Monte Kwinter, Bill Bernbach, Rob Myhill, Stan Freberg, David W. Smith, Julian Koenig, the late Sam Goldberg, Bruno Rubess, Woody Herman, Harold Livergant, Michael Burns, Peter C. Newman, Bud Turner, George Sinclair. The list is endless. Oh, how lucky I am.

Joyce Seidel-Goodis

FOREWORD

I heard the name "Jerry Goodis" for the first time way back in 1957. The four syllables of his name were uttered by a mutual friend, the late Carl Dair, one of the great type designers. It was Carl who designed and created the first distinctive Canadian typeface, Cartier. It was Carl who set up the Typographical Designers of Canada. It was Carl who sparked the formation of the Guild of Hand Printers.

But this foreword is about Jerry. When I knew Carl he was still a partner in the team of Goodis, Goldberg, Dair. Whatever happened to Goodis, Goldberg & Dair? According to the Corporations Act, companies are supposed to be immortal. It must have gone the way of all companies that are too small to excite big bankers. All I know is that thereafter the company became Goodis, Goldberg, Soren. In this book we learn about that company. But I never had the chance to ask Carl about his involvement with Jerry. At fifty-five, in the Centennial Year, Carl died of a heart attack.

There is no mystery why Carl spoke well of Jerry. Carl recognized genius when he saw it. As well, Carl was a former printer and like many printers he leaned somewhat to the left. And in those days, and perhaps even in these days, Jerry leaned somewhat to the left. I honestly have no idea how Jerry votes, if he votes at all, but I do know that he was a founding member of The Travellers. This now legendary pioneer folksong group grew out of Camp New World, a leftist, Jewish trade-unionist summer camp in Ontario in 1954. I never saw The Travellers perform in concert, but I saw them on television, heard them on radio, and listened to some of their albums. Their signature song was the Canadian version of Woody Guthrie's "This Land Is Your Land". It still makes my heart beat stronger to remember those words about this land being "your land" and this land being "my land" — all the way "from Bonavista to the Queen Charlotte Islands".

So Jerry was a genius to Carl and a legend to me. Over the years I read interviews with him and articles by him; I heard him on radio; I saw him on television; I even watched a one-hour NFB film about him. I read his book *Have I Ever Lied To You Before?* and enjoyed it. Here was a leader in the advertising industry in Canada, an industry that is always interesting to watch, if only as the bellwether of social change. Jerry was an unabashed Canadian nationalist, a man with a social conscience, an innovator who put creativity foremost, a man willing to speak out and be heard.

In those days, Jerry was Peck's Bad Boy. At industry awards occasions, he excoriated the excesses of his peers and colleagues. He criticized the commission system, preferring instead the fee system. Some members of the industry were critical of Goodis and suggested that he couldn't run a business profitably so why should he knock the profitable operations of others. But when he spoke, he made loud sense and the headlines. Here was the man who spelled his name on his letterhead with an exclamation mark: "GOOD!S". Here was the guy who gave the English language a new comparative and superlative: Good . . . Gooder . . . "Goodis". Jerry's campaigns and penchant for personal publicity were good for the industry. I hope they generated some business for Jerry's agency of the day. But I suspect some salvos scared off as many clients as they attracted.

I met Jerry for the first time in 1986 in the office of Avie Bennett, the developer who was then installing himself as the publisher of McClelland and Stewart. Avie and Jerry, it seemed, were old friends, both being native Torontonians. Suddenly there, in the flesh, was Jerry: this little gnome of a guy, spiffily dressed, deft of movement, exuding energy and awareness, the spitting image of his publicity shots!

It was a luncheon meeting and for the first few minutes it was like Old Home Week. We jabbered about Carl Dair, about typography, about advertising, and about books. At one point Jerry asked me about my ancestry. "Colombo? That's an Italian name. Are you Italian?"

"Not really," I replied. "The name's Italian, of course, but I'm only one-quarter Italian and I don't speak the language."

"What's the other three-quarters?"

Then I replied, not for the first time, "Ethnically, my four grandparents are Greek, German, Italian, and French Canadian."

I paused to allow Jerry to murmur some piety about ethnicity or multiculturalism. But he surprised me with an apt and completely original comment. "Funny," he said, "you don't look it."

It was at that point that Avie interrupted us, and we got down to the business of the day, which happened to be the design and promotion of one of M & S's books. Jerry had no end of inspired ideas about launching the book. My recollection is that none of his concepts *was* ever put to use.

I suppose that's a difficulty Jerry faces every day. I wonder if he loses hours of sleep over it. Someone may be an idea machine and a phrase factory, even the centre of attention, but unless someone else is willing to go to bat, the spit of ideas and the polish of phrases go to waste. The words languish in some limbo of lost souls. No doubt Jerry has a memory bank full of spectrelike concepts that were never embodied in campaigns. Yet his success has been phenomenal in bringing concepts of quality to market and in the process endowing everyday products and services with a kind of animistic power.

There are two characteristics of his concepts. First, they are fun. They are enjoyable — not annoying — commercial messages. Secondly, over the years his concepts have turned into urban folklore. They have wide appeal and application. Jerry is a copywriter of genius, the finest that Canada has produced, certainly one of the best in the world. As well, he is unfailingly quotable. The public knows his words, if not his name. He has worked, sometimes alone, sometimes with other talented people, on the following familiar advertising campaign slogans. Most Canadians will recall them the way they do old friends:

"At Speedy You're a Somebody"

"Buy Canadian. The Rest of the World Does" (Hiram Walker)

"For 3 Bucks You're Laughing" (Canadian National Exhibition)

"Get Your Head into Hush Puppies"

"Harvey's Makes Your Hamburger a Beautiful Thing"

"If We Hurry Our Beer, We'd Lose Our Heads" (Formosa Spring Brewery)

"Quick! The Elmer's Glue."

"Salada Tea Picks You Up and Never Lets You Down"

"We Care About the Shape You're In" (Wonderbra)

"Never So Good for So Little" (Swiss Chalet)

I limited myself to quoting ten. Many more of his phrases are firmly planted in the Canadian psyche.

And now to the present, and to Jerry's new book. Again he has chosen a rhetorical title. He's never lied to us before; he may have told a fib or two, but no outright lies. What can he tell us now? Something new? He can, and does tell us much that is new and interesting. He is particularly informative about advertising, agencies, corporations, businesses, governments, politics, salesmanship, commercials, the media, consumerism, consumer concerns, sexism, stereotyping, discrimination, social conscience, Canada, and people. Above all, he tells us what makes Jerry Goodis run.

I think I can epitomize the book and the man's appeal in a single phrase.

"With Jerry, You're a Somebody." (and so is he!)

John Robert Colombo

INTRODUCTION

A Couple of Cracks in My Crystal Ball

I wrote my first book in 1972. It was the year "The God-father" won an Academy Award for best film, and Roberta Flack won a Grammy for her single "The First Time Ever I Saw Your Face". My book didn't win any awards but it was called *Have I Ever Lied To You Before?*

I didn't just dream up the title. It came from the pay-off line in a television commercial we produced around that time for Borg fabrics. Picture the scene since you probably don't remember the ad. A little, wizened garment cutter is explaining the merits of the goods, as they say in the trade.

At the end of the 60-second commercial, he says: "How do you know you're getting the real Borg, and not the imitation? Simple. Just look for this label." Then he spreads his hands in the classic Yiddish gesture and asks: "After all, have I ever lied to you before?"

The client loved it. The public loved it. It helped sell Borg fabrics. It helped sell my book. But that was then — and now is now. Eighteen years later, I look back on that title and wonder: Was there an intimation that, although I'd never lied before, I was about to stray from the truth in my book?

Not really, but I must admit I did say a few things then that make me blush a tad now when I see them in print. Just a tad, mind you. For instance, in talking about account executives and senior creative people in advertising, I did write: "For some reason, very few of them are women. Probably creeping male chauvinism." Probably, my foot! Creeping, my toosh! Flagrant!

But, thank God, in the ensuing two decades, that attitude has all but disappeared. Even hardnosed "ad men" — well, maybe with a few exceptions — now admit that the female of the species has all the intelligence and moxie needed to handle any account, any marketing strategy; and the talent and creativity to write, design, or produce the best in advertising. I've worked with two dozen in my career who are world-class talents!

Of course, that doesn't mean that women have yet reached an equal plateau with men in the hierarchy of the ad game. They're on the move. More power to them. No longer can any ad agency ignore the fact that women have become a major purchasing power in our society — not just of female products, food, and children's items — but of almost any goods and services you want to name. And if you want to attract those buyers, then you had better have a hell of a lot more input from women when it comes to planning campaigns and creating ads.

In my 1972 book I stated my belief that the commission-payment system, where an agency is paid a percentage of advertising placed in the various media (generally fifteen per cent) was "about as appropriate to today's business conditions as a Model A Ford is to today's super-highways".

I still believe that. The fact is, however, that most agencies haven't relinquished the system. Don't even want to relinquish it. It was the most profitable way to bill then — and still is — even though it's totally self-serving. Why should anyone get paid strictly on the volume of advertising when its effectiveness in the marketplace is its true measure of value? An imaginative, inexpensive campaign, used wisely, may boost sales significantly, yet the agency only gets paid on the amount of money spent. On the other hand, a massive, dull campaign may have little impact on buyers. Still, that agency is laughing because it's just increased its income substantially. That makes sense only to the agency.

The problem I face is that I never totally abandoned the commission system myself, even as committed to the overall merits of a fee-for-service plan as I was. And still am. With fees you win and hold clients through merit, not volume of expenditure. Obviously, it's not always easy to maintain your principles in the face of day-to-day realities and circumstances. Nor is it ever easy to change the status quo, even over almost two decades.

Now, however, since I've become the self-appointed *eminence grise* of Canadian advertising, re-asserting those principles in the cause of fairness to both advertisers and the media, as well as to the eventual well-being of the advertising agencies themselves, is one of the tasks facing me in this book.

I also stated — somewhat unequivocally — it was my opinion that "The trade paper (those that are directed at readers in specific industries or businesses) as we know it hasn't much longer than ten years left." Well, that prophecy was, perhaps, a little premature. Although, in the interim, some trade publications have evolved to meet the needs of their readers, there is still an abundance of badly written trade mags, grinding out inordinate profits from advertisers on the leaky-boat theory that, if you have a large enough mailing list of business names, readership is guaranteed. Balderdash!

Cartoon presented to Jerry Goodis on the occasion of The Jerry Goodis Agency attaining billings of $20 million. Artist: Gray Abraham

With the advancement of the electronic age — more correctly, because of it — business publications rank far down on their list of priorities, if they rank at all. Skimming briefly through the pages of a magazine is not what I call the best climate for getting your advertising message across.

Of course, there are a number of exceptions to this observation. *Marketing* Magazine is read, cover to cover, by advertising, sales and marketing folks every single issue. It is an institution in that industry, not just a weekly gossip sheet. Some medical trade magazines, hospitality magazines, and journals which serve the paper and wood industries are read with gusto by those in the industries to which they cater. But exceptions or not, the trade magazines, in my view, continue to be repetitive, self-serving, and, by and large, so beholden to their assigned sectors that they hesitate to critically editorialize sensitive subjects or problems facing their brethren.

And I still believe the trade mags are in deep trouble. Back then, however, my conclusions were based on the following premises. First, that their obvious lack of quality would prove to be their undoing. Secondly, the availability of justifiable alternatives would win out over the uninhibited rush of advertisers to support any vehicle that simply stated it was directed exclusively at a captive audience.

I even went so far as to say I believed business trade shows would replace many trade publications. Little did I realize the two, to a frightening degree, would come to work hand-in-glove, living off each other in a near-incestuous relationship. Ah well, stranger things have happened in this business. Some of the trade shows are owned by the very same publishers of trade magazines in their particular industry. We used to call it "vertical integration".

But that's it. That's all I wrote then that brings, in retrospect, even the slighest blush to my face. Not bad, almost a generation later. On the other hand, many of the topics I dwelt upon at length in that book are as significant and vital to advertising today as they were back then.

I still believe originality, clarity, and freshness in its creativity is the very foundation of all good advertising, despite the lack of it in so many ads you may hear, see, or read nowadays. Give me an idea, a fresh original idea for a print ad, a TV commercial, a billboard, a radio spot. Please, someone, an original idea! I also believe, as I wrote in '72: "A series for Crest toothpaste makes me ashamed that I have anything to do with the industry. It's the one where the kid runs in to interrupt his father at work shouting, 'Daddy, daddy, only two cavities.' The father stops what he's doing to discuss toothpaste."

That commercial has now gone through its second generation, with child-actor graduates saying: "That was me back then"; and, like their actor fathers — long cavity-stricken — going on to discuss the same old toothpaste.

As I said in my book: "That Crest series is bad advertising. I don't care if it increased market share of the product by five per cent. I wouldn't care if it had increased market share five hundred per cent. Any approach to the consumer that is intrinsically low-minded — tasteless or offensive or patronizing or cynical or insultingly silly — devalues all advertising." Even if the client buys the concept for more than eighteen years.

All it proves is that bad advertising breeds more bad advertising. But, thank God, good advertising also breeds good advertising. After all, our line: "At Speedy You're a Somebody" is still around, too. The difference is: Ours was true — and still is. It wasn't based on a Cinderella concept that insulted the intelligence of the buying public. Speedy Muffler King delivers the promise their current (albeit dull) advertising makes to us viewers.

And how about this description of beer commercials back in the early seventies: "The music was bouncy rock. The dramatis personae looked like chorus-boys and chorus-girls. . . . The costumes were golf-club-casual with hairbands for the girls and open-necked shirts for the men. The photography was full of swish-pans, and creative one-up-manship which came in dreaming, tilted angles. And of course in the swingingest activities (beach partying, bobsledding, water-skiing) or most ingenious settings (midstream on a dam, out on a lighthouse). . . . I have never understood how the ordinary beer-drinker bringing home a case or ordering in a beer parlour is supposed to relate to these goings on."

Look and sound familiar? Of course. Except for a few updatings of clothes, music, and scenery, more refined technical pizzazz, and more Vaseline around the camera lens for mood, they're the same dumb macho commercials today.

And, if you look at them closely, the women have little else to do other than serve beer and food, open fridge doors, stand in awe of the male heroics, or bob up and down on the dance floor. They're just requisite background to the male scene. Like hockey pucks.

I knew who the principal target audience for beer commercials was then — and it certainly doesn't appear to have changed much in the ensuing years. At the same time, there have been a few campaigns that proved to be an exception to the rule. The 1989 Black Label one, for instance, comes to mind. Palmer, Bonner, an agency of superb craftmanship and blessed with the guts to try something different, created it. It used splashes of dramatic color against black backdrops full of abstract images to register its revitalized name as strongly as possible. It makes one hope. But the more I look at this industry of mine, the more I wonder when it's going to go through a creative revolution. Advances in technology, it seems, inspire present-day ad types more than good, original creativity. Just fax me an ad, guy.

At the same time, perhaps I wasn't strident enough, back in '72, especially in the chapter called: "The Yankees Are Coming!. The Yankees Are Coming." I wrote then: "Don't be fooled when you read about mergers between Canadian and U.S. agencies. It would be as appropriate to speak of a merger between a cannibal and a missionary. . . . How long can the dwindling all-Canadian-owned agencies hold out against the blandishments of the U.S. giants? I don't know, but even card-carrying optimist Jerry Goodis is pessimistic on this score."

If I was pessimistic then, I'm distressed now. And it's not just the Yankees. It's the multinationals from wherever. The essential problem isn't simply the corporate takeovers themselves, although they're bad enough. It's the insidious creative bludgeoning. That's where the culture of the multinational thrusts itself upon every country — including our own — in the layouts, copy, storyboards, and final production of so-called universal ad campaigns.

Typical of this trend is a recently introduced campaign for a new Gillette razor, called the Sensor. Worldwide, the budget is reportedly in the neighbourhood of two hundred million dollars. The frightening thing is that the same ads are going to be used in more than twenty countries, from

Canada to Japan, from the United States to Italy. Are we living in that much of a global village? Are we all becoming that identical? The U.S. may think so — doesn't it always — but anyone in Canada knows better. Quebec and Ontario are not the same. The Atlantic provinces are distinctly different from the prairies. Now broaden that worldwide. Global advertising campaigns may save money on production but it's nothing short of foolhardy and self-defeating to attempt to foist the same creativity on a wide assortment of varying cultures.

Myself, I'm sick and tired of ten-gallon hats, California-style kitchens, Florida beaches and swimming pools, continental-European restaurants, Venice-inspired fountains, and a plethora of ad symbols that say little or nothing to anyone in Charlottetown, Trois Rivières, Kincardine, Le Pas, Swift Current, Red River, or Trail, let alone Montreal, Toronto, Winnipeg, Edmonton, and Vancouver.

I have a yacht. But the background against which I sail has nothing to do with what I see in universal lifestyle commercials produced by multinational agencies. Absolutely nothing. I can't even recall seeing an evergreen or a maple in full fall colour in any of them. It's all palm trees from the South, certainly not here.

We are a country whose essential foundations have been established in the beauty and diversity of our multiculturalism and multinationalism; a blend of all the small things that make us uniquely who and what we are, set against a backdrop of the inherent majesty of our country. That should be reflected in our advertising as it is in other areas of day-to-day living. Most of us — or our parents — came to Canada to start a new life, a better life, not to ape the one we left behind; or envy someone else's.

I may have been mistaken at times, but: Have I ever lied to you before? No.

And I'm damned if I'm going to start lying to you now.

CHAPTER ONE

If I Was a Cat, I'd Have Nineteen Lives

I've been involved in three mergers during my career in advertising. I guarantee you I'll never get involved in another one again as long as I live. The first was in 1975 when I exchanged my shares in Goodis, Goldberg, Soren (GGS) for those of MacLaren Intermart Inc., the holding company of MacLaren Advertising. The second occurred in 1983 when the Jerry Goodis Agency (JGA) joined Wolf Advertising Ltd., and the final one was last year when Goodis & Sharabura (G & S) shuffled off unceremoniously to Lowe Case Associates, owned by McKim Advertising.

The initial merger was the result of egotism and greed, the second came out of economic necessity brought about by the recession in the early '80s, and the final one because I'd lost interest in the business. One lasted four years, another three months, and I didn't move with the last. To be quite frank, they didn't want me. Nor did I want them.

I suppose, throughout all these events, I should have known better. The problem was that it was so easy to be swayed by one argument that kept cropping up in my mind.

When merger mania began, I began ranting and raving about how terrible it was, especially when a Canadian agency was taken over by a U.S. or U.K. firm. I was the ardent nationalist. In fact, I still am. I'd had numerous foreign companies come and talk to me about joining with them. I turned every one down. Throughout my first merger experience, though, I kept telling myself that I was joining with another Canadian agency, so it was alright. Despite what other counsel I received, this argument kept popping up in my own mind and convincing me to do it. So I did.

Yet the biggest mistake I ever made in my advertising

career was going to Intermart and MacLaren. The second biggest mistake was leaving it. In 1975 when George G. Sinclair, the chairman and CEO of Intermart, approached me with an offer to join them, my company, GGS, had annual billings of about ten million dollars, and a lot of clients who had been with us for years. At the same time, MacLaren was the largest agency in the country with combined billings of more than seventy-five million. In fact, in the business, it was known as Mother MacLaren.

When the approach was made, I was stunned. What the hell did they want with me, the so-called enfant terrible of the business? After all, this was THE WASP establishment and I was simply — to quote others — the poor little Jewish boy from the wrong side. An incident, one that occurred only a short time before the approach to me was made, graphically illustrated how far apart George Sinclair and I were.

At the banquet to celebrate *Marketing*'s advertising awards the year the merger was struck — but before we had even begun to negotiate — George was the main speaker. In his address to the more than five hundred guests — myself included — he reviewed Canadian advertising over the past ten years. *Marketing* said about his presentation, it was "smooth, polished, erudite, and entertaining". It might have been entertaining to most, but it wasn't to me. Although indirectly, he said some nice things about our agency, he also levelled some harsh criticisms at us. I was infuriated. At one point, I vaguely remember rising up from my chair. I am sure I wasn't going to punch George in the mouth. Maybe I was about to storm out; or, as I said later to people who asked, I was going to ask for equal time. No matter. Doug Linton, our creative director — and to become GGS president after the merger — pulled me down by the sleeve. Doug, in a loud stage whisper, enjoined me to "cool it. He's an old putz whose time has come and gone — he wishes he were you. Just drop it and stay put. . . ." Doug prevailed; I stayed put.

The fact is I was incensed for days. And everybody knew it. The nerve of that bastard to criticize us. Who the hell did he think he was? We could out-create his agency any day. So he had some flattering things to say about us. So what? He also cut us up in front of our peers. And on and on until the storm passed and I could finally get my mind back on business. Then, some five months later, George and I got "married". Bud Turner, the president of Intermart, acted as both marriage broker and best man.

Now I look back and wonder what would have happened if Doug hadn't grabbed me fast enough? Or hard enough? I don't mean about that particular night, but about GGS and the rest of my career. The funny thing is that, when the deal was consummated, George said in his public statement: "I have always seen Jerry Goodis as the most interesting competitor in the Canadian advertising business. I've admired most of his work — some of it immensely. I've admired Jerry's courage in speaking out on contentious issues. Of course, some of his public statements have irritated me more than a little — others I've admired." Here we were merging and he was still taking subtle potshots at me. A couple of months before, we'd have been in a contentious issue alright. With him on the receiving end.

For my part, I admit I was in seventh heaven. My statement was, I guess, typical of my gadfly reputation, "A friend of mine laughed when I told him the news. He couldn't tell which one of us was getting in bed with the devil. I said it didn't matter since we were going to have such a hell of a lively time together. I thrive on excitement. I like making new things happen. And Jerry Goodis at MacLaren is exciting. Crazy, but exciting. Different. Beautiful. There's a theory that every boy wants to marry his mother, and I've done it."

I used to say such things. I still do, though perhaps with a little more reserve. Even the *Time* Magazine article on the merger was headlined "Marrying Mother". The fact is that I got along well with both George and Bud. Never once, that I can recall, did we really lock horns. The same couldn't be said of others at MacLaren.

What you have to understand is that, while MacLaren acquired GGS, both retained their identities. The reason for that was simple. Some clients wanted the more conservative approach of Mother Mac, others desired the adventurous creativity of my firm. The move also made economic sense to both companies. MacLaren had the best media department and research group in the business. Therefore, as everyone agreed, the merger offered loads of room for greater efficiency. A combining of services would go a long way in placating clients who were demanding more and more for their buck every year.

GGS itself was on the rise, at that particular time having achieved billings in some fifteen years that no other Canadian agency had come close to. But the business was changing. Growth was not as fast in the early seventies, for either company. The marriage made eminent sense. It would allow us to concentrate our efforts on capturing new clients, rather than competing against each other. And, as far as GGS was concerned, it could expand its support facilities without the costly extra overhead.

When the deal was struck, I essentially left GGS and moved downtown to be Vice-Chairman of Intermart. George, Bud, and I had equal shares in the company. In combination, I had bolstered my ego and satisfied my desire for guaranteed security. What else could I ask for?

Well, I'll tell you, and it says a great deal about my state of mind at that time. Intermart pandered to my every whim. I wanted a chauffeur-driven Cadillac. I got it. I wanted a sumptuous office. I got that, too, and did a lot of redecorating. Back then, I was floating in a dream world. I believed it was true that the boy from Toronto's Bathurst and College, who had grown up poor during the depression, was now at the top of the world.

For the first couple of years, everything went well. I prided myself on client relations. GGS billings under Doug Linton, Lee Master, and Al Blugerman grew, so did MacLaren's. Everything was looking rosey. What happened then, during 1978, is a matter of some contention. The trigger — in my mind anyway — was the fact that GGS needed me at a certain point and I wasn't physically there to help. The first indications came via subtle messages. Hiram Walker, GGS's biggest account, hinted that it might leave if I didn't return to having a hands-on role. So did Speedy Muffler King.

I reported all this to what I called the GGS troika: Doug Linton, managing director Lee Master, and Al Blugerman, the chief financial officer, who, incidentally, was my cousin. They pooh-poohed what I said, arguing that it was just normal client discontent, which would pass. So I went back downtown to MacLaren Intermart where I had lots to do. After all, the GGS billings had almost doubled in the first couple years after the merger. Maybe they knew more than I did. They were far more involved in the agency than I was.

The fact is, I was right. I take little pride in saying that.

I should have followed my initial instincts. Both Hiram Walker and Speedy switched agencies. In short order, so did Alcan and Consumers Distributing. Now, of course, the fat was in the fire. The Intermart board began to panic. It had one solution. I had another. Doug Linton resigned. The board wanted to send Marty Rothstein, a senior vice-president at MacLaren, up to Don Mills, where GGS resided, to replace Doug. I wanted to go myself. In the end, after much wrangling, the board won. The argument against my going was that I had too many clients to handle downtown, including a lot of Federal Government business.

When Marty arrived at GGS in early July 1979, all hell broke loose. Lee Master resigned and the Rothstein purge of the staff began. Some people say it was the biggest in Canadian advertising history, at least until then. Within a few months, almost half the staff got the chop.

For most of the purge, I was also at GGS. Only a short time after the board sent Marty, I decided to move into an office uptown at GGS and try to resolve the situation. My intentions were honourable; the result was a disaster.

Rothstein and I had never gotten along from the first day I joined Intermart. He had been at MacLaren for years and he resented my coming in and superseding him. He told me so on a number of occasions. To make matters worse, our philosophies on advertising couldn't have been further apart. We should never have come within a continent of each other, let alone within the same business. That three or four months was a nightmare to me. GGS clients were like my own children. All I wanted to do was to help keep them, to bridge the creative and administrative sides of the agency. I didn't do it. Marty kept chopping away and I kept flailing about. The irony was that I was Rothstein's superior. I could have fired him, but I didn't. All we did was fight.

I had never been under such pressure. It was a war zone. When people — my people — got fired, I hid from them. For instance, John Edmunds was a superb senior account supervisor with GGS. He'd been there for years. He got the axe and I avoided him. To this day I don't know why. As with Don Quixote, I preferred to fight the windmills rather than face reality. It's one of the few times I've been truly ashamed of my own behaviour. My intentions were good, but they weren't good enough to salvage anything.

Nevertheless, I refused to retreat until I was exhausted. I don't remember what touched it off. One day I decided to leave Intermart. Bud Turner was away on vacation. I sank further and further into myself. Some people were kind enough to say the reason was that my marriage was shaky; I had lost much of my zeal for MacLaren-like corporate duties; and that Jerry Goodis should really be on his own where jealousies and rivalries and petty bullshit don't occupy half his day. Lots of truth to those issues. Basically, however, I had turned a blind eye to everything but getting out. I still kept swinging at Marty but it was nothing more than the reflex action of a punchdrunk fighter. Finally, I sat down with Bud. I told him I wanted out. He told me I was crazy, which was probably closer to the truth than he knew. The more he argued with me, the more adamant I became. In the end, I just walked away.

In retrospect, I should have listened to him. I should have taken a vacation and come back to handle MacLaren's business alone. But I wanted to return to my old ways. I wanted to take clients through the whole process, not just up to a certain point, then leave them to others. In my own agency, I had worked that way — right through the creative process, and beyond. At Intermart I hadn't learned to separate functions, as must be done in large corporations. I liked to be captain of the team. I loved directing the creative process, but hated the administrative side. My past caught up with me at MacLaren, and I never learned to adapt.

But that was a mistake, too. I should have grown. I should have thought it through from the beginning — and changed. I didn't and it caused me, perhaps, to miss the brass ring. I would have succeeded Bud Turner as chairman of the board had I opted to stay. It also caused a lot of pain to others, which is what happens when you selfishly hang on to what you are comfortable with, with what pleases you. And, maybe, with what you do easily. When I graduated in art from Central Technical Collegiate in Toronto in 1949, I began to freelance. One of the people who gave me work on a regular basis was Sam Goldberg, the production manager at Muter, Culiner, Frankfurter & Gould, a medium-size Toronto agency. I wasn't a great artist, not even a good one, but I put a lot of effort into what I did. And the agency seemed to like the results. One day after I'd done work for them for three or four years,

Eddie Gould, a partner in the firm, called me into his office and offered me a job. The salary: $7000 a year.

I nearly fell off the chair. Here was I, a kid almost fresh out of school, and Eddie was offering me the world. I don't think my father had ever made that much in his whole life. I decided I'd better discuss this with my stepbrother, Albert Soren, who is a chartered accountant. Albert said: "If they want to offer you that much, then why don't you go into business for yourself?" Now I was really confused. But the more Albert talked, the more I liked the idea. He even suggested that I approach Sam Goldberg as a potential partner.

The upshot was that Sam and I started our own agency with very little money, but with a great deal of desire. I quickly found I was an aggressive salesperson; Sam excelled at production and administration. Al Soren looked after the books, and eventually joined to become Goodis, Goldberg, Soren. As the agency grew, I found I had a natural flair for what clients wanted and a way of communicating that to creative people. Perhaps because of my background: my radical youth, my love for working people, my sensitivity to things cultural — Canadian or otherwise, and my continuing political involvement gave me a feel of what was needed to trigger warm feelings and desires in the people to whom we were advertising. I knew instinctively whether an ad would accomplish what we wanted or not. I wasn't right all the time. Far from it. But I was right often enough.

From the beginning, however, I was excluded from the financial and administrative sides of the agency. I was inadequate in these areas. I couldn't decipher a simple financial statement. "Do what you do best," Sam and Al told me, and don't worry about the rest. Therefore, I never learned the slightest thing about the rudiments of business. I never even thought about them. My partners corralled me into one area and I threw all my energy into it while ignoring all other aspects of the business. They didn't do it intentionally. It was just that I was so inept at some things; far preferred to do others. As I look back now, that was a big mistake. I should have taken an interest. I should have learned. But when you are successful beyond your wildest dreams, who cares? That lack of foresight, that imbalance in my training and experience caused me a good deal of grief when I moved to MacLaren. I was too used to having it my own way.

The money and the perks at MacLaren bolstered my ego. I had all the confidence in the world about getting new accounts. What else would I need? As you have seen, a great deal more. Of course, if Sam hadn't died at age forty in 1967 and Al hadn't retired in the early seventies, there would still be a GGS. That doesn't mean I didn't have good people around me during the intervening years until the merger. It simply means I didn't learn, even when my partners were gone.

Much of my public reputation was built on the fact that I stood up to clients successfully right from the start. As part of my presentation, I told them I wasn't going to write ad campaigns to please them, but to woo and win their potential customers. It worked. Not every time, but, at least, when clients came on board, they knew where they stood with us. Too many agencies don't do that. They simply pander to their clients. Therefore, I got a reputation in the outside world as being a tough-minded creative leader.

The more that reputation spread, the more I was asked to publicly speak on advertising, the more I was asked to comment in the news media. I gobbled that up too. It fed my insatiable ego, and it helped our business. Many clients, fed up with the bootlicking of others, came to us. We welcomed them. At the outset I didn't seek such notoriety. It was just that I couldn't keep my mouth shut under certain circumstances. Under any circumstances, really. If you asked me a question, you got an answer. I didn't seek speaking engagements; they sought me. I didn't phone the media, or send out press releases; they came after me. Once I was out there, I loved it. I didn't write my first book on spec; I was asked to write it. When the National Film Board wanted to do a one-hour television documentary on me, I was surprised. But they wanted to do it. And so I did.

I was a media puppet. All you had to do was dangle a question and I jumped. Reporters and broadcasters came after me for a "quotable quote". Ultimately, especially as I became more involved in politics, the questions began to go well beyond advertising to practically any subject imaginable. Need an opinion? Goodis has one.

Much later — in 1987 to be exact — Colin Muncie, the editor of *Marketing*, told a story about me in an editorial. "There was a lunch some years ago, when that gadfly Jerry Goodis was at his peak as a critic of the advertising business, at which the godfathers of three advertising agencies offered me a bribe to keep Goodis out of the pages of *Marketing*. 'How much,' one asked me, 'how much would it take to keep him out of *Marketing*?' 'There's only one way I know to silence Goodis,' I replied, 'and that's by standing up in public to answer his charges. If you do, *Marketing* will report what you say. But we will continue to print what Goodis says as long as it is news our readers want to read.' The lunch (they paid) then ended rather abruptly."

I'd love to know who those three scumbags were. I can guess, but I won't. But such was the state I had the Canadian advertising world in. And I loved every moment of it.

I've said some pretty outlandish things in my time. What I didn't realize then was that, in a way, I was being suckered. Whatever came easy to me, I specialized in. I shook aside anything that was difficult. Well, you just can't do that and be able to run a business properly. With Goodis, Goldberg, Soren, I had two trusted friends to protect me. At MacLaren, I still acted as if there had been no change. I never adapted. I've learned to, but it took me a hell of a long time, as well as a great deal of suffering. It also cost me a lot of money.

My second merger was an even greater disaster than the first.

Within six months of leaving MacLaren, I opened up The Jerry Goodis Agency Inc. This time I was going to do it right. The Goodis touch was going to become the Midas touch. I had the proceeds from my shares in MacLaren, although that wasn't as much as it could have been. I did the resignation negotiating on my own behalf. It should have been someone else, but my jerk lawyers and accountants at the time advised me I should do it face to face. It was yet another mistake because I'm not a good negotiator. And I had lazy lawyers and auditors who sent me, alone, to do the negotiating. Idiots.

Our opening shot for the new agency was a full-page advertisement in *The Globe and Mail* on December 5, 1979. The headline read: "This Advertisement Isn't Good Enough." The copy read in part: "It can't be. It was created for a client who will never be satisfied — a perfectionist who believes there is always a better way, who believes in going the extra mile. That client is us. We're a new, full-service advertising group, The Jerry Goodis Agency Inc., dedicated to serving clients who share our deep determination to excel. We believe

YOU DON'T HAVE TO OUTSPEND THEM. JUST OUTFOX THEM.

Times are tough.
Maybe even terrible.
Your advertising has to work. Has to work harder than ever before.
Has to cut through the clutter.
To provoke.
To cajole.
To nudge.
To move.
To impress.
And always, to sell.
Which isn't simple, but not impossible.
And you don't have to outspend your competition, you just have to outfox them.
Which can be done by caring.
By giving a damn.
By your agency understanding the difference between an ad that just runs,
and an ad that works.
By your advertising being impactful and potent, rather than safe and dull.
And that's what we do, every day, some sixty of us, at The Jerry Goodis Agency.
We search.
We find out who we're talking to and make them _feel_ something.
We don't just impart information—that's journalism—we go for the heart _and_ the head.
We go, always, for the big idea. The ad or TV spot with originality, artistry, memorability.
The special something that sets your product or service apart from your competitor's.
And we go for incisive positioning
coupled with the sensible use of research and shrewd media planning.
We go the last mile, full out.
No altruism here. The more we can do to help our clients through times like these,
the better things will go for our business also.
Right now, as you read these words, we have clients making money,
doing well, in spite of the economic climate.
Efficient, effective advertising is helping them outfox their competition.
Which makes right now a good time for you to call Jerry Goodis, to get together,
one on one, to find out who and why and how.
And whether we can do it for you too.
The number's 416-863-0500
We have the people, and the drive, and the enthusiasm, and the imagination
to make your advertising work harder than ever before.
Because we truly give a damn.
One last thing.
Sure it's easy for us to say.
We have the satisfied clients to prove it.

Amicare Inc.	Extendicare Ltd.
A.E. LePage (Ontario) Limited	The Financial Post
The Bank of Canada—	Freidberg Mercantile Group
Canada Savings Bonds	Holiday Rent-A-Car System
The Bank of Nova Scotia	Mr. Submarine Limited
Canada Post Corporation	Savin Canada Inc.
Canadian National Exhibition Association	Syncrude
C.N. Tower Ltd.	Canada Ltd.
Cochrane-Dunlop Limited	Systemhouse Ltd.

GOOD!S

The Jerry Goodis Agency Inc.
130 Adelaide Street West, Suite 2100, Toronto, Ontario, Canada. M5H 3P5 Telephone: (416) 863-0500.

the very best clients are the most demanding. And the most they can demand is the very best. We know they're the ones who will survive, indeed thrive, in the challenging times ahead. . . . The Jerry Goodis Agency profoundly believes that it takes both a good agency and a good client to create powerful advertising."

The rest of the copy outlined what we were looking for in clients. The signature was: "Goodis. The best is yet to come." We sweated months over that ad created by Jim Hynes and the wonderfully talented Robert Burns, changing the copy, then the headline. Again we reached consensus — and it ran. The result? We were off and running. Clients joined up rapidly, good ones at that. CN Tower, *The Financial Times*, King Edward Hotel, Syncrude, Scotiabank, A.E. Lepage, MAI Canada Ltd., to name a few. I went after the Federal Government and got business out of it (after all, I was an ardent Liberal and had worked hard on a number of election campaigns). By March of 1980 we had close to five million dollars in billings and fifteen employees. In only three months. By the end of the year we were closing in on ten million.

Then the recession of the early eighties started to squeeze us, especially as Ottawa began to cut back on advertising expenditures. I still had my confidence, but needed more capital to get over the economic downturn. It was provided by Harold Livergant.

I had met Harold just after I opened JGA. Curiously, we were at the same tailor — Stavros on Church Street in Toronto — for a fitting. We were introduced. He gave me his card, and asked me to phone him. That's how we got the Extendicare account. Harold was chairman of the board. Later we became friends and, at one point, I discussed my cash flow problems with him. His company had just acquired Crown Life. Harold said they were interested in further diversification. He suggested a meeting with Michael Burns, chairman of the board of Crown Life.

After this meeting they decided to invest in my company. A holding company, Caldonia, was formed and Crown Life, the umbrella organization, purchased forty-nine per cent of the shares. Harold, who is an astute businessman, was intent on building a communications conglomerate. At one point during this period, his company also held a substantial

THE BUMBLEBEE CAN'T FLY.

According to the theory of aerodynamics—in terms of wing spread in relation to body weight —the bumblebee cannot get off the ground. No sir.

But, the bumblebee (bless him), refuses to get caught up in the theoretical, and does indeed fly. And for that matter, helps make a bit of honey too.

We at The Bank of Nova Scotia think there's a lesson in this for all of us. For we have believed in the Canadian dream for 150 years, and we think it's time we all stopped getting caught up in uninspiring economic theories that indicate failure.

This country of ours was built by people, determined people, who were not stymied by unknown geography and a sometimes most inhospitable climate.

And as our country grew and expanded, so did the aspirations of our individual people—people who refused to admit that their ideas wouldn't fly.

People like Banting and Best who were determined to find a way to end the suffering of diabetes.

Or a man like Van Horne who insisted that a railway could and would be built from sea to sea.

Or a woman like Celia Franca who believed that this country should have a ballet school that was equal to any in the world.

And Emily Stowe who opened the Ontario Medical College for Women—determined that women could become doctors.

Or a man like Alexander Graham Bell who envisioned that one day using a telephone would be second nature to us all.

Look at the Columbia. That's a Canadian arm— a Canadian solution—hard at work on the space shuttle.

In almost every field of human endeavour that you can think of, there have been, and there will be Canadians who have or will overcome obstacles in their path. And succeed.

We know of a businessman (he's not even a customer of ours) who talked with several advisors about his plans to open a jewelry store. Everybody advised against it. Bad location. Not the right time. Caution. A lot of caution.

He believed in his idea and opened up and his business is booming, truly booming—in spite of the economy.

We're not suggesting that everybody should now go out and open a store against all advice.

We are suggesting that we should get back to believing in our ideas and our plans and our dreams. And in Canada.

Scotiabank

WE'VE BELIEVED IN THE CANADIAN DREAM FOR 150 YEARS.

Scotiabank — writer Mark Levine, art director Gray Abraham — The Jerry Goodis Agency Inc.

interest in Cockfield, Brown, a large, Toronto-based agency that was in serious trouble. Eventually that company broke up, but, of course, Harold had backed off at the right moment.

By the middle of 1982 we were in the midst of the recession. Perhaps a merger with another agency would consolidate our billings and give us additional strength? It could also

"THE SKY IS FALLING"
SAID CHICKEN LITTLE.

And a lot of people believed him for a while. Until (thank goodness) it was pointed out that what had hit Chicken Little on the head wasn't sky at all, it was just a small acorn.

Now these days, a lot of people believe that the country is falling apart.

And because we at Scotiabank have been a part of this country for 150 years, we think it is really important to point out that while the economy is not in very good shape, it is not all over, finished, kaput.

But most of the reports—what you read in the papers, what you see on TV—seem to us to be leaving the impression that the situation is almost hopeless.

Which only adds to the fear and pessimism.

Sure times are tough. But we've believed in this country before it even was a country.

This year, we're celebrating our 150th anniversary. And through the millions of Canadians we've met and dealt with, we've been left with a positive and optimistic outlook for the long term.

Canada is still rich in resources, and richer still in people.

Our institutions are basically sound and stable.

Most of us have been through tough times before. And made it through. And we will again. We're going to make it.

Maybe we should all start acting that way.

Scotiabank

WE'VE BELIEVED IN THE CANADIAN DREAM FOR 150 YEARS.

be a step forward in establishing the basis for the conglomerate. About the same time I brought in Adrian Eaves as president of JGA so I could concentrate more on getting accounts and overseeing the creative process. With a possible merger in mind, I began having discussions with Lawrence Wolf, president of Wolf Advertising Ltd. I had known him for a number of years, well enough to have dinner with him and his wife a few times. He had always been charming. I

21

"OH, WHAT BEAUTIFUL CLOTHES THE EMPEROR IS WEARING."
SIGHED THE CROWD.

That crowd certainly had the wool pulled over its eyes. They'd heard so much about the Emperor's new clothes, so often, they became blinded by the publicity of it all.

Until of course, a child pointed out that the Emperor was as naked as the day he was born.

Now these days, we're of the opinion a lot of folks are being blinded by the publicity—the non-stop publicity—of how bad things are.

And because we at Scotiabank have been a part of this country for 150 years, and because we believe in it so strongly, we are determined to make the point that Canada has the resources and the people to make it through these tough times.

Furthermore, we feel that a constant negative attitude tends to accomplish nothing—except to instill the feeling that there is little or no hope. And we don't believe that this is the case.

It is not a no-hope situation.

Through the people we've met and dealt with over the years, we've been left with a much more positive outlook than can be gleaned from the media these days.

True there are no instant, easy solutions.

We're all having to tighten our belts. But it is not the end of the world.

Sure times are tough right now, but we'd like to point out that this country's institutions are basically sound and its citizens basically strong. And resilient.

And capable of making it through.

And the sooner we all start remembering that, the better.

So hang in there.

We all can do it.

Scotiabank

WE'VE BELIEVED IN THE CANADIAN DREAM FOR 150 YEARS.

respected his reputation in the business as a talented writer and an excellent marketing strategist.

The talks began to heat up between us with the encouragement of Crown Life. Neither one of us (nor any other agency) was getting much new business. If we combined resources, we would have a formidable base that could carry us across the twenty-million dollar threshold in billings. When we got down to serious negotiations, I began to

"A WOLF! A WOLF! A WOLF!",
CRIED THE BOY

True, when the crunch finally came, nobody believed him. But more important is how many people did believe him when there wasn't a wolf for miles.

Nobody really checked it out at first. They just believed the boy. And panicked.

These days, a lot of people are crying wolf and gloom and doom.

And because we at Scotiabank have been involved in this country of ours long before it even was a country, we are determined to point out that while everything isn't perfect, there's a lot to be optimistic about.

For example, we might not like high interest rates, but at this point in time there is strong evidence to support the fact that they are doing the job of helping to curb the inflationary spiral.

And while the economy is far from fabulous, in actual fact, Canada is in better shape than most countries today.

Yet the focus seems to always be on how bad things are. Which adds to the fear and pessimism.

At Scotiabank we think it's time we all acknowledged that times are tough—but we're going to get through them.

This year, we're celebrating our 150th anniversary and through the people we've met and dealt with over the years, we've been left with a much more positive feeling than can be gleaned from the media these days.

Even for times like these.

For Canada is still rich in resources and people. People who are strong enough and tough enough to not throw in the towel.

Sure we're having to tighten our belts.

But we'll all make it.

Let's start acting that way.

Scotiabank

WE'VE BELIEVED IN THE CANADIAN DREAM FOR 150 YEARS.

see another side of Larry Wolf that I hadn't known existed. It wasn't just that he was a tough negotiator, but he started to show a personality that I can only describe as insensitive, even brutish. It bothered me at the time, but I shrugged it off as part of the pressure of the bargaining process.

I also made another error in judgement. I didn't listen to my lawyers, who made me sign a document stating they couldn't be held responsible for the merger because they were in disagreement with it. Would I never learn? They couldn't bear the sight of Wolf, and were fearful of what he might do to me. Eventually, in the Spring of 1983, a number of events came to a head. Three out of the four weeks in March we were the streamer story on the front page of *Marketing*. I don't know if anyone else has ever achieved that.

On March 7 the headline was: "Goodis president quits after six months." Adrian Eaves just hadn't worked out. Adrian came from the culture of a large agency. He is bright as hell, articulate, erudite, but had a hard time tuning his style into our aggressive environment.

On March 14 it was: "JGA takes home a golden awards trio." That obviously pleased me. These were the magazine's own awards. Undoubtedly the most prestigious in Canada. To take three of the five top honors spoke well for our creative output. We had beaten out the big boys creatively — in single radio spot, radio campaign, and black-and-white newspaper advertising. Neither MacLaren nor GGS Ltd. (the name was shortened to initials after I left) were anywhere in sight. *Marketing*'s headline on March 28 read: "Goodis and Wolf decide it's time they both got their acts together." Looking back on that edition now, I wish I **had** gotten my act together.

In the story, I had little to say, which was a distinct change. On the other hand, Wolf summed up the merger this way. "Jerry is the seminal creative person in Canada. He is really the guy who brought Canadian advertising into the 20th century. If we combine Jerry as a creative resource with the disciplines of our packaged-goods orientation, then we create a very formidable resource." The only problem was, that as soon as I took over the combined Goodis-Wolf agency as chairman and CEO, and Wolf as president and chief operating officer, events confirmed that my partner was not a sheep in Wolf's clothing.

Within a few weeks, I realized he was trying to take over the company completely, including my own clients. He scheduled meetings with them without my knowledge. He tried to convince them of things we had never discussed between us. Whenever I was out of the office, he rifled through my files, taking what he wanted. He tried to shut me out. When I returned home from one business trip, my secretary informed me that she had caught him in my office going through my desk. Just what the hell was he up to? Then the Bank of Nova Scotia, one of my better clients, phoned to say "We can't put up with him anymore. You've hooked up with an animal." I was shocked. I hadn't even known they were meeting. When I confronted him, he just shrugged it off.

The last straw occurred one day a couple of months into the merger. I heard an uproar in the creative department and went to see what was happening. Wolf was berating one of my art directors. I physically had to separate him from the poor man, whom he had the nerve to call "a talentless, English working-class bastard." That was it. The pressures were too great. I had to seek psychiatric help. My doctor told me never to go back to the company. The dilemma I faced was that the agreement was iron clad as far as my clients' commitment to the new agency was concerned. To make matters worse, my name was incorporated into it as well. Finally, Crown Life was deeply involved financially.

Eventually, when I recovered both physically and emotionally, I sued Wolf for wrongful dismissal and settled out of court. But later I had to buy back my *own name* from him at some expense. And Crown is still suing Lawrence Wolf for the money his company owes it. Wolf tried to take over the clients, the employees, the styling of the shop. I found out about meetings after the fact, my secretary had caught him rifling through my files and he made it clear, through his actions, that he thought I was the John Diefenbaker of the agency world. I was in a fury. I sued him and I won.

All I had wanted to do was join with someone so that I could seek out clients and look after the creative end. I thought Wolf was a good fiscal administrator. Although I didn't know him well, it had seemed to me to be an ideal match. I didn't have the slightest idea I was marching into the cave with Dracula. I should have listened to my new legal advisers, but a lot of things were happening, both good and bad. I was caught up in the potential of our combined agencies. Greed again? Perhaps, but not as flagrantly as in the case of MacLaren. Ego? Sure, but I wanted the rebirth of the strength of Goodis, Goldberg, Soren and thought I could find it with Wolf. Never could I have imagined the three months of hell I went through with him.

How did this guy Goodis ever survive in the business as long as he did? Good question. The answer is simple. I got along with clients well. They trusted me and I trusted them.

I don't think I have ever had a client pull a dirty trick on me or my companies. I also had good working relations with the vast majority of my staff. Again, mutual trust was the foundation of our relationship.

Looking back now, I believe my major weakness was that I trusted **everyone**. Although that is better than trusting nobody, one should, at times, exercise a little restraint; a small cocking of the head that says: Wait a minute. Let's step back and look at this in perspective. I didn't do that. When someone said something to me, I took their word as gospel. I had absolute trust in them. I believed in consensus, especially where creativity is concerned. That means you trust the people around you and their opinions. You know they are not bullshitting you.

The problem I had was that, when people became untrustworthy, I didn't react appropriately. I couldn't see through them. At MacLaren, I trusted George Sinclair and Bud Turner, and they never let me down. Others, I couldn't say the same about. At Goodis-Wolf, there was only one person I couldn't trust. I never realized it until it was far too late. But I should have been able to see through these people. I just could not. I trusted everyone — and hoped for the best.

In the midst of my depression during 1983, there was only one bright spot. At the time, I didn't know whether it helped or hurt, but friends used it to bolster my spirits. They probably knew best. In the September 23 issue of *Marketing*, Canada's leading creative critic, Ted Wood, chose his ten most favourite ad campaigns stretching over a period of twenty-five years. That meant he was going back to 1958 as a beginning to pick out ads that, as he said, "stood the test of time". I wasn't even out of high school then.

Guess what? Goodis had three of the ten. In second spot in Ted's ranking was Speedy Muffler. He said of the line: "one of the best and longest-lived ideas to come out of a Canadian agency". In fourth spot was Elmer's Glue. And, in sixth, a London Life campaign that Ted said "was literally all heart". The creative forces behind them were, respectively: Oscar Ross, Oscar again, and Doug Linton.

When I finally got out of my blue funk, I launched Commonwealth Systems Inc. as an advertising consulting business. The staff was small, and although we did some good things, I spent more money than I had. Within two years the company folded. I lost my beloved yacht ("Midnight Sun"), a portion of my art collection and a lot of cash, including my RRSPs. As I told *Canadian Business* a few years later: "I went from the top of the industry for twenty-five years to the sidewalk below, bleeding and emotionally hurting." But it wasn't the same as my experience with Wolf. I was able to rebound much better. I was still handling more than two dozen speaking engagements a year, and doing some consulting work for people I knew — and trusted. In 1987, I phoned Avie Bennett, the relatively new owner of the book publishing firm, McClelland & Stewart. I had never met him, so it was a cold call. That didn't matter. I had heard that Bennett was a gentleman, very clever, astute, and liberal in his thinking.

Full-page newspaper ad for publisher McClelland & Stewart produced by Jerry Goodis Inc.

We hit it off from the beginning and everything I had heard about Avie was absolutely so. We became friends. Soon he and I were discussing the establishment of a new company; one that would concentrate on providing a broad cross-section of integrated services that I believed would be the new wave of marketing and advertising in the future. We would build the business, not upon advertising per se, but

Globe and Mail *full-page advertisement for Goodis &* *Sharabura Inc.*

on strategic marketing and communications. That may appear to be a fine distinction, but it isn't.

After numerous meetings, Avie and I came to an agreement. With his financial backing and space provided by him in the same building as his publishing firm, I was in business again. Michael Warren, a close friend, joined the board of directors. Richard Sharabura, an advertising man with a

---

Pierre Elliott Trudeau

1001 BOUL. DE MAISONNEUVE OUEST
SUITE 1400
MONTRÉAL, QUÉBEC H3A 3C8
(514) 281-1212

September 30, 1988

Dear Jerry,

    Great going, Gospodin!

All good wishes,

Pierre Elliott Trudeau

Mr. Jerry Goodis
Deputy Chairman of the Board
Goodis & Sharabura Inc.
Suite 502
481 University Avenue
Toronto, Ontario
M5G 2E9

Letter from The Right Honourable Pierre E. Trudeau

broad experience in many of the newer aspects of the business, joined the firm as a partner. What had begun as Goodis, became Goodis & Sharabura Inc. in May 1987.

As always, we started off well. We got clients. Why not? I was the deputy chairman of the board (Avie was chairman) and executive creative director. Richard and I wrote the firm's bible, an 80-page book that began: "This handbook is dedicated to those decision makers who are prepared to break out of the prison of past assumptions and to forge ahead into the brave new world of virtually unlimited marketing opportunities."

We brought in Alistair Beattie from Ogilvy & Mather as president of the firm. Richard initiated an acquisition program that was, initially, successful. But our growth was too slow. I take partial responsibility for this. It was more difficult to explain our philosophy to clients who were used to the old ways of marketing. New accounts didn't come in fast enough to keep our balance sheet balanced. And, perhaps, I began to lack the verve I had shown earlier.

In November 1989, a merger was arranged between our firm and a McKim division, Lowe Case Associates. Alastair went with the new company. Sharabura had left the firm earlier, a victim of his own indiscretions. Richard Sharabura had been asked by the board for his resignation. Poor Richard had left a trail of resignations and defeats behind him for "indiscretions, misbehaviour, and questionable fiscal tactics" — all of which I was warned about before inviting him in as a partner. I, in my usual arrogant manner, ignored the warnings, wanting only to see his good side and turning my back on his bad side. Chalk another one up on my list of misjudgements, my insatiable desire to trust everyone. And Jerry Goodis? I'm here. Rarin' to go again. But no more advertising agencies, no more mix and matches. I'm working with some people in some ventures — those people I trust implicitly, and those ideas I know I can bring to fulfillment.

I am now working with my best friend and wife, Joyce, as a partner in The Jerry Goodis Partnership, Inc. We have interests in business which Joyce manages and shepherds through the maze of meetings, re-scheduling, banking, travelling, and fulfilling of commitments.

One exciting venture we are deeply involved in is Goodis & Hughes, a company practising "venture marketing" — a new method for serious marketing professionals to be doing business. David Hughes and I have invented a concept called Venture Marketing, in which we combine our expertise and marketing resources with venture capital. We become, not merely a marketing consultant, but a partner, measuring our success on bonuses linked to performance and accountability, and taking an equity position in our client's venture. In some cases we are the client's marketing department. In others we will work with a client to a certain point and then select an agency. And yet in others we are client and agency combined. In all cases we share the risk, the rewards, and responsibility.

A final word on the personal career of Jerry Goodis. I've been described as the gadfly of the business, an iconoclast, the bad boy of advertising, the self-proclaimed conscience of the business, a professional phoenix, a charismatic, intuitive salesman — even an anachronism. How many epithets can one human being have? I've even been described by my friend Peter C. Newman as a self-made man who worships his creator.

Just after Goodis & Sharabura opened its doors, I was invited to speak at a management conference. By happenstance, that same morning there was a mention of me in a *Globe and Mail* gossip column. In effect, it said I was attempting my sixth comeback. What was I going to say to the conference? I told my audience: "Where do they get six comebacks?" I sent a telegram to *The Globe*. It said: "Fuck you. Strong letter follows." They loved it. Adversity is there to be beaten. And, dammit, it makes us better people.

I know that, too.

CHAPTER
TWO

Caps Off to Sam Slick,
That's Right, Sam Slick

I'm a fan of Thomas Chandler Haliburton. If you don't know who he is, you should. Every Canadian should.

Thomas Chandler Haliburton came from a distinguished Nova Scotian family and, during his lifetime, served as both a Member of Parliament and Supreme Court judge in his home province. But, as commendable as those accomplishments might be, they're not the prime reason you should know his name. The fact that he invented the character Sam Slick, of Slickville, is why he should be remembered, revered, and studied by every generation of Canadians.

Why, you may ask, is this so important? Because, through the mouth of Sam Slick, Haliburton gave us a wealth of wise and witty sayings that are as true and appropriate today as they were in 1835 when Sam first made his appearance in Joseph Howe's Halifax newspaper, *The Novascotian*. His wisdom and insight into the human character were formidable and thought-provoking.

Furthermore, Sam Slick may have been the original marketing guru in Canada, despite the fact he was fictional — and a Yankee. That is why I have come to love him. He wasn't simply an itinerant clockmaker, but a genius at marketing. He represented the quintessence of door-to-door selling, an entrepreneur who could talk his way into your home, sell you a product, and leave you happy that you had known him — and purchased his wares. He not only had the gift of gab, but a practical wisdom and a creative touch that made his sales pitch, not only irresistible, but an enjoyable experience to the people he came in contact with. He was a man who recognized "The Big Idea" and how important it is in getting your message across to consumers.

Soft Sawder & human natur

London Published by Richard Bentley 1848

If only our present-day advertising pundits could come close to emulating him, advertising might be hailed as a gracious and insightful art form, rather than condemned as a confusing swirl of images and sounds that we must endure in order to obtain basic information on products and services we may — or may not — want.

Among the more inventive aphorisms that T.C. Haliburton put into Sam's mouth, and have become household sayings in almost every corner of the world, are these: Seein' is believin'. — Facts are stranger than fiction. — You can't get blood out of a stone. — An ounce of prevention is worth a pound of cure. — It's the early bird that gets the worm. — A miss is as good as a mile. — There's many a true word said in jest.

And the one I should have remembered at various points in my career: Hope is a pleasant acquaintance, but an unsafe friend.

And these are just a few of his better known contributions to our language and culture. All of them, of course, you recognize immediately. What you probably did not know was that they were born in Canada in the fertile mind of Thomas Chandler Haliburton.

It seems only fitting, then, that I sprinkle this book with Sam Slick phrases that are pertinent to the subjects I wish to discuss, and what I want to say about them. In fact, I can think of no better marketing mentor in Canada than Sam. And he is more than a hundred and fifty years old.

Let's get something straight right from the start. As maligned and denigrated as marketing and advertising are now, they are vital driving forces in our society. They are the creative energy that makes the economy go. Without them, the world of business and industry would not function as effectively as it does.

Therefore, it is ironic that, when I am introduced socially as an advertising man, often people look at me suspiciously as if they aren't sure they want to meet me, or even shake my hand. They're not certain they wish to be associated with a so-called "huckster", a man who wants to sell them a second-hand car, or a set of encyclopedia. They have this vision that I am plotting against them, sizing them up to pick their pockets.

And, sometimes, if they deign to speak with me, they

invariably thrust some time-worn morality onto me, like: "Do you ever worry about what you do: about seducing people into buying something they probably don't need, or can't afford, and which generally doesn't fulfill the promise they expect from it?"

That is when I go into my little spiel. It goes something like this: "If somebody has this great idea for a product, what do they do? First, they find the financing to perfect and produce it. Then they hire people to manufacture it, and other people to sell it. But, if they don't market and advertise it well, hardly anybody is going to know it exists. And, if no one knows it exists, no one is going to buy it. And, if no one buys it, then the financial shareholders are going to lose their money; and the people the firm hired are going to lose their jobs. Therefore, my colleagues and I perform a public service. Without us, there would be a lot of pain and suffering, not to mention the fact that all those people associated with the product wouldn't have the cash to buy the things they want."

Depending upon the person or persons I am talking to, I can make the explanation softer or harder. I can even sprinkle it with expletives if I think the situation warrants it. No matter. When I am finished, I politely excuse myself and look for more congenial company.

The fact is, of course, that a significant number of people think this way — and you can't change their minds. They have a holier-than-thou attitude, regardless of the fact that they are as influenced by marketing and advertising as anyone else. I'm influenced. We all are.

Why then, do people have this attitude? Quite simple. There have always been outspoken critics of advertising, just as there have of other professions. But criticism of ours has been heavier, nastier. It has been called "the permissible lie", "the half truth", "the seduction of the masses". Critics have stated ad nauseam that: "All advertising is inherently misleading."

I concede that there is some misleading advertising. But that's unscrupulous marketing and, when people find out about it, the product or service generally goes down the tubes. There are laws to protect the public against such false advertising. Far more evident in our profession is bad marketing, bad advertising, created by professionals who are incompetent. Yet one finds incompetence in every discipline. Why is ours always tarred and feathered with impunity?

The problem the marketing and advertising profession has is that it is involved exclusively in the art of persuasion, which many believe is the soul brother of propaganda. And we all know the connotations attached to that word: Fascism. Brainwashing. Intolerance. Bigotry. The truth, however, is far different.

Before the industrial revolution, only the rich could be considered consumers of products and services other than the bare necessities of life: food, clothing, shelter. And whatever the rich wanted, they had individual artisans make for them.

Once the industrial age was in full swing, however, products began to be mass produced. That required a larger consumer market. Not to anyone's surprise, the market came from the very workers who were doing the mass producing because, now, they had the money to make purchases other than the essentials. And marketing and advertising were born as integral functions for communicating the merits of those goods and services. Eventually, as more and more such products became available, competition grew for the consumer dollar. That brought about more marketing, more advertising. It was the only way to move product off the shelves more effectively — more profitably.

Now, of course, since society has reached heights of affluence unknown before in history, we have an even greater abundance of products and services available to us. Why? Because the human being is — and always has been — an inventive creature with an equally driving ambition to succeed by developing new and better products to attract our interest, or more intriguing services to cater to our needs, or better ways to make our lives more pleasurable. In other words, a better mousetrap under numerous guises.

Who, among us, does not strive for such achievement, such success? Show me anyone with an ounce of enterprise in them — just an ounce — and I will show you a fully functional human being. The car, the airplane, the telephone, the radio, the computer, the fax, the television receiver, CD player, video tape; each is a primary example of such inventiveness and ambition in the fields of transportation and communications. And all were developed by individuals, working almost exclusively on their own. And each eventually needed marketing and advertising if the result of their work was to be brought within reach of the vast majority of us because, only through volume use, could most of us afford them. Point made?

Furthermore, it was the upsurge of advertising that played a pivotal role in the growth development of the mass media and made them easily accessible to the whole of society. Without ad revenues, newspapers and magazines would be prohibitively expensive. The wide range of radio programming would certainly not be possible. And television would be mainly a rerun of movies and documentaries.

In Canada today, there are more than 100 daily newspapers with a total average daily circulation of 5.3 million copies, reaching approximately 50 per cent of all homes. Advertising makes their existence viable. The newsstand cost of the paper doesn't come close to paying the freight. The only reason you pay is so that readership can be measured, and ads priced on the basis of that circulation.

There are currently more than 700 radio stations covering the whole of the country, and more than 120 television stations reaching 99 per cent of the population. With few exceptions, both these media are equally dependent upon advertising revenues. And I haven't mentioned general and specialty magazines, or community newspapers. Total advertising expenditure in all these media by only the leading fifteen national advertisers exceeds half a billion dollars per year. That is a hell of a lot of funding and support, and it's only the tip.

What this inexpensive accessibility to the media means is that, as a people, as a nation, we are better informed about what goes on around us. We are better entertained — at least most of the time. We are more knowledgeable about everything from business to government, from sports to weather, from music to drama to war in the Gulf. And the vast majority of it is funded through the profits generated by mass marketing and advertising.

As the Special Senate Committee on Mass Media, chaired by Senator Keith Davey, pointed out in its final report: "Because value is received, it is unfair to describe advertising as a form of subsidy to the mass media. What is not only fair but vital to realize, however, is that advertising is the overwhelming, the first, the chief source of revenue for the media. Our research indicates that sixty-five per cent of the gross income of all newspapers, and ninety-three per cent of the gross income of the private broadcasting industry comes from this source." While, admittedly, these figures were compiled in 1970, I have no reason to doubt that they are fundamentally accurate twenty years later. There just isn't any other new source of revenue that has come to the fore during the interim period of time.

I make no apologies for my profession. It is an honourable one, with as many skills and disciplines as the others. And, like other professions, it can boast of its achievements, its traditions, its breakthroughs, and its setbacks. Admittedly, there is probably a greater degree of ineptness in marketing and advertising, but that is because it depends more upon intuitive creativity and instinct than upon formal process and rules. And it is more self-taught through hands-on experience, at least at this point in time. But these, in themselves, make it unique, challenging.

This book is not an apology for the profession of marketing and advertising. Far from it. I've written it for a number of reasons.

Primarily, I believe as many people as possible should have a knowledgeable grasp of the inherent skills, techniques, and motivations involved in my profession. Only in that way can they understand what we do. Only in that way can they make more conscious, intelligent decisions in a world that offers an overwhelming number of choices. And only in that way can they approach the marketplace with unrestrained confidence. In essence, I believe an informed public will make us more responsive to the needs of our audience, the consumer, as well as to the needs of our clients.

Furthermore, I would like to see the profession ascend to heights never before achieved. That would require significant changes in the way we now go about our business. It would require a re-assessment of such important facets of the art as creativity, media, research, planning, budgeting, and client relations. And, if we are to accomplish it, we must do it as a co-ordinated profession. Only in that way will we be taken seriously.

As my friend Sam Slick said: "There is a way of doing everything, if you only know how to go about it." Let's find out how to go about it. You will have noticed that I have invariably paired the terms "marketing" and "advertising". Are the two identical? No, they're not. The fact is that, while they have always been inter-related, until recently they have been considered separate and distinct disciplines.

No longer, however, is that appropriate to either. The more complex the world has become as far as the number of goods and services available to the public, the more the two have become an integral part of the same function. No marketing strategist can develop a product profile without considering the advertising possibilities and ramifications; no ad agency can develop a campaign without having intimate knowledge of, and input into the marketing plan.

Let me give you a simple example, the automobile. Not too many years ago, there was only one Chevrolet model. If you wanted a Chevie, you simply went out and bought one. Now you have a choice of the Chevrolet Sprint, the Cavalier, the Corsica, the Beretta, the Celebrity, the Astro, the Lumina, the Camaro, the Caprice, the Tracker, and, of course, the Corvette. Eleven models under the same family name; all with spin-off variations; all seeking to attract a certain segment of the market through price, styling, and an array of individual features.

Confusing? Perhaps. But, in today's marketplace, one has to position one's product to find the appropriate niche of like-minded buyers. If you do not, someone else will seek out the niche to your disadvantage. And that is why marketing and advertising are becoming, in essence, one discipline. Without an integrated strategy, combining the skills of both, chaos would result. The product more often than not, would fail. The service dismantle.

To develop the point even further, let us briefly look at the present dictionary definitions of "marketing" and "advertising".

Webster's defines "marketing" as: "An aggregate of functions involved in . . . moving goods from producer to consumer including, among others, buying and selling, storing, transporting, standardizing, financing, risk bearing, and supplying market information." That sounds all-inclusive, but is it? Let's delve a little deeper. The first thing we notice is that it excludes the manufacturing process, which is appropriate since that doesn't fall under marketing. On the other hand, it also excludes design, packaging, and pricing, all inherent marketing functions.

The fact is that the dictionary definition of "marketing" just has not kept up with the realities of the present-day marketplace.

Now, let's look at what *Webster's* has to say about "advertising": "The action of calling something to the attention of the public, especially by means of printed or broadcast paid announcements." That is just too simplistic. It might have been true thirty or forty years ago when the world was a much simpler place. Now it begs too many questions.

How about these for starters?

• What about the name and personality of the product or service, a function of both marketing and advertising?

• What about positioning the product to attract those buyers for whom it was intended?

• What about the selection of which media to choose in order to reach those buyers more selectively?

• What about the expenditures required to do the job thoroughly?

• What about, once one has made an impact, retaining the market share you have developed?

• *What about the creativity that is required to make that impact on prospective buyers in the first place!*

Although the dictionary definition of "marketing" is skewed because of rapid development within the field, the "advertising" definition is practically neanderthal. Why? Because the advertising profession has matured by leaps and bounds as the demands upon it have increased dramatically. On an average day, there are more than a hundred advertisements in a metropolitan daily newspaper, excluding the classified and career sections. There are more than two hundred spots on a typical radio station, and about the same number on a TV channel. The vast majority of these ads are for different products and services. All are competing against each other for attention. All are attempting to gain recognition with the reader, the listener, the viewer. All are bent on convincing you to be a purchaser.

Naturally, every product and service is not for you. For instance, pet food. It is marketed almost exclusively on TV because that medium offers the most graphic way of presenting the furry, household creatures in the best light. If you don't have a pet, you don't give a damn about the food they eat. Still you have to put up with the commercials. The only thing they might do for you is to convince you to go out and buy a cat or dog. But that is only a sidebar to the true purpose of the advertising campaign. What it really wants to do is get at pet owners in the most cost-efficient, persuasively effective manner. And that takes talent, or, rather, all kinds of talent.

As more and more products come onto the market — and there are thousands introduced across Canada every year — the greater the competition for your attention. Therefore, in order to be successful, the combined efforts of marketing and advertising have to be good.

It is a tough, demanding profession, and getting tougher by the minute. I love it. I have always loved it. It's half science, half art. It is a dose of psychology mixed with a heaping cupful of statistics. It is knowing how to use a budget to get every ounce of impact from it. And, above all, it is creative instinct, knowing how to get to a purchaser's head through his or her heart, which is a slight adaptation of another Sam Slick saying: "The road to the head lies through the heart."

What else can I say? Well, lots. As I said earlier, there is good advertising and there is bad advertising. There is silly advertising and there's poignant advertising. There are tried-and-true techniques of persuasion and there are inventive new ones. There are old media and new computer-age ones.

And there are the advertising people themselves. Before we get into the techniques, applications, fallacies, and opinions on advertising, let us look briefly at what leaders in the business had to say about it entering the '80s and what they foresee for the future. When you create an advertising campaign, you have to get to know the product or service as well as you can so that you are comfortable with it. Hence, a little background — and comment — on what was said then and now.

CHAPTER THREE

The Future in a Rear-View Mirror

Marketing Magazine is the bible of the advertising industry. It works well as a business publication for two reasons. First, it publishes mainly news about the profession, articles you are unlikely to find in any other medium. Secondly, it is a weekly, which means its news is more or less timely. And there is always lots of news in the ad world.

Marketing is also sado-masochistic. It depicts within its pages all the triumphs and defeats, the blood-letting, the scourging and beating of breasts that are inherent in the cut-throat world it covers. If a million-dollar account — or a fifty-million-dollar one — is won or lost, it reports that. When people are hired or fired, when they decide to quit or set up their own shop, when someone wins an award or goes bankrupt, you can read it all in *Marketing*.

It is also the favoured vehicle for people in the business to take scathing shots at one another as if they were involved in a religious pogrom, although most of bombast deals almost exclusively with someone else's lack of creative skill or even common sense. It is wonderful, but you have to be in advertising to fully appreciate it. No other field — other than those of fashion and entertainment — delights so much in savaging its own, much to the glee of everyone who is not being gored. I know the feeling.

At the beginning of each year, *Marketing* presents the views of the various segments of the industry on what is going to happen in the next twelve months — or ten years if the year ends in zero. To accomplish this, editors and reporters ask for the opinions of certain eminent leaders of the profession. It is supposedly a privilege to be asked, but it is really a penance for being successful or heading up one of the industry's numerous trade organizations.

Now, what I have done is study the 1980 forecasts as reported by *Marketing*. I have tried to determine whether those predictions were fulfilled, and, if not, why not. I have also looked at the forecasts for the decade of the '90s.

First, let's step back to January 1980. Advertising executives were looking toward the new decade with outright optimism. They predicted it would be one of exciting and dramatic change, of giant strides that would benefit the whole industry. There were, of course, some fears, but these were mainly based on the possibility of government intervention in what the business could or could not do.

In retrospect, this elation was somewhat surprising since, at the time, Canada was struggling through a minority government with a supposed lack of stability. There was also the threat of a fuel-oil shortage and higher gasoline prices, as well as strong indications that the economy was heading toward a recession. It didn't matter. All the predictions were bright and rosey for advertising. The TV bureau projected increased ad revenue, the newspaper associations called for increased ad linage, and the advertising industry predicted bigger spending by clients. It was as if the industry was determined to buck any negative trend, no matter what others saw in their crystal balls.

Most of the optimism was based on one single factor. There was a great deal of talk about "space-age communications", whether that involved satellite communications, fibre optics, cable TV, or any number of other technological advances. Nearly every expert from Bud Turner, chairman and president of MacLaren Intermart, at the time Canada's largest advertising agency, to Peter Swain, president of Media Buying Services, talked about "an explosion of technology" and "an era of space-age gadgetry". There was even speculation that — soon — we would have a hard-copy newspaper delivered via cable TV on a home teleprinter. It was as if advertising had found a new god to worship.

Many of these predictions came true, although whether they truly benefitted advertising to the extent the forecasters expected is a moot point. Yes, we now have TV programming by satellite, which allows viewers a greater diversity in what they can watch. That variety of choices also makes it infinitely more difficult for marketers of products and services to select where they are going to get their biggest bang for a buck. Perhaps that is why, as predicted in the same issue of *Marketing*, computerization of media selection would be one of the major changes in the business. That, of course, has happened. It is akin to one technology desperately trying to catch up with another technology.

And, yes, we do have fibre optics, which allows for expanding communications links using minimal transmission conduits, as well as cable TV. Again, however, their impact on the advertising world has not been nearly as dramatic as the seers intimated they would be. It's as if they heard about all these innovations and suspected — or hoped — they would have an enormous impact.

On the advertising revenue side, there seemed to be little cause for trepidation either, even though the recessionary fears prevalent then were about to come true within a short period of time. The billion-dollar target figure seemed to be favoured by the pundits because it undoubtedly sounded impressive. "Ad revenues of one billion projected for dailies in 1980" was the headline over John Foy's forecast as the general manager of the Canadian Daily Newspaper Publishers' Association. The medium didn't quite make it that year, but broke the barrier for the first time in 1981 and has really never looked back. "Radio eyeing a billion in the 1980s" was the projection by the then president of the Radio Bureau of Canada, Jim Adam. The target was surpassed easily within the decade.

Since inflation in the early eighties was rampant, it is almost impossible to determine whether these forecasts came true because of marketing incentives or by way of the escalating costs of advertising. Still you could not deny the enthusiasm.

Strangely enough, there were no predictions concerning revenues for television, although there was an article on pay TV, which was just being introduced to Canadians. Why TV was not included is beyond me, since it was, even then, considered the Midas child of all the media. To top it all off, one estimate by the magazine publishers organization overreached itself immeasurably. The article forecast that advertising dollars would shift to mass-reach magazines because of the escalating costs of TV ads. It was written by a spokesperson for *Canadian Weekend* magazine, which is no longer, of course, in business. So much for forced enthusiasm.

While optimism reigned supreme, certain aspects of the business were left in limbo, not to be discussed. What was missing in all this hype was the major trend in advertising during the past decade. That was merger mania, which I will discuss in greater detail later. The trend toward it was well underway. Therefore, either nobody wanted to talk about it, or they just could not foresee what an impact it would inevitably have. And, I truly suspect, no one at that time could have predicted that the grande dame of Canadian advertising, MacLaren Intermart, would be a victim of merger mania before the decade was out.

There was no mention, either, of the increasing role of women in advertising. There was an article on the difficulty of college graduates getting into advertising because agencies only hired people with packaged-goods experience and would not take a chance on the eager but inexperienced. This thoughtful piece was by Julian Clopet, president of Ogilvy and Mather. He called the problem "packaged-goods snobbery". His only mention of the female sex, however, came at the very end of the article when he summed up his optimism for the future by quoting the old adage: "Faint heart never won fair maiden." And, by the way, Ogilvy, one of the leading U.S. agencies, would be gobbled up by merger during the ensuing ten years.

Is nothing sacred?

Nor was there any mention of *creativity*. It seemed to be totally ignored in the rush to jump on the technological bandwagon. Certainly any change in advertising production technology has a profound effect on the creative process; but, without the craftsmanship of those who write and design the ads, such innovations simply become toys that soon pall on viewers, listeners, and readers. But there was no critique of where creativity was in 1980 or what challenges lay ahead. Technical gadgetry reigned supreme. To a large extent it still does, but whether it contributes significantly to good advertising or is a crutch for the indigent and unimaginative is something that has to be looked at in far greater detail.

Two final predictions should also be noted. The first was made by my good friend, MacLaren's Bud Turner. "New advertisers will appear with contemporary goods and services," he wrote "in a world of greater conservation, more intelligence, and dramatically revised needs." It didn't happen to the extent it should have in the '80s, but it's beginning to come true now. The other was made by Larry Foley, chairman of McKim Advertising, Canada's oldest agency, which was also involved in merger with a U.S. company in the '80s. He said: "It is highly likely that advocacy or issue advertising will grow as a category as business leaders decide to advance their viewpoints in a controlled environment and to counter criticism and attack from various strata of society and special interest groups." He was bang on. The only area of influence he missed was that of governments. They would also get more and more into advocacy as both policy and social issues demanded greater exposure to the public.

It is easy to look back ten years and criticize what was said then in relation to what would happen. My intention in doing so is not to take shots at my colleagues, but to establish a basis for delving into the theories and processes that have been prevalent in my business for a good number of years and, to a large extent, still dominate it. And a perspective on the past is always required in order to judge the present. Even more so to look into the future. And, speaking of the future, what do the advertising leaders see in their crystal balls for the '90s? If the '80s predictions were full of lofty enthusiasm, the '90s are almost bereft of optimism. And I have difficulty understanding this. There are problems, but they are by no means insurmountable. Certainly there is uncertainty, but there is challenge and opportunity as well . . . recessionary cycles notwithstanding.

I get the distinct impression from looking at the most recent predictions that marketing and advertising is in a state of disarray. If such is the case, it has only itself to blame. For quite some time now, it sat back and ignored many facts of life, coddling itself on gimmickry and gadgetry. It could be compared to a child who is only happy if it has a new Nintendo game to play, but has no idea about how to enjoy itself if left to its own devices, the back-to-basics that have made children the imaginative and inventive creatures they have always been. And always will be.

I was startled at the pessimism when I read *Marketing*'s "Forecast '90" issue in early January. Collectively, the headlines give one a feeling of despondency. Individually, they are more problem-prone than solution-oriented. "Creative heart at risk." "Some tough sledding ahead for the daily newspapers." "The trauma in the magazine trade." "Agencies continue down a rocky road." "Future bleak (for retailers)." "Outlook remains grim (for commercial production)." That's the stuff of doom and gloom.

There were some upbeat forecasts, especially for television, radio, and a few of the ancillary media: outdoor advertising and weekly newspapers. But the overall impact was one of negativism. I hope Keith McKerracher's comment in his projections on behalf of the Institute of Canadian Advertising has some validity. In part, he said of his own predictions: "If any of this makes sense and it may not because we're all terribly bad at foretelling the future. . . ." One hopes that he was speaking for other forecasters as well.

Many of the problems were, naturally, laid at the door of the Federal Government, especially its Goods and Services Tax. There was also, understandably, fear of a possible recession, which finally did strike. In contrast, however, to the upbeat enthusiasm of advertising people in 1980 (when all indicators pointed to a significant downturn in the economy), the despondency of 1990 (when there were, at most, mixed signals as far as a future economic slowdown is concerned) is like Chicken Little.

Myself, I hope that the advertising industry is simply going through a cathartic stage, not a catatonic one. Some of the inherent problems of the industry are given their due: merger phobia, traditional creativity, consumer appreciation, but mainly in a superficial way. It is as if, although they are beginning to understand where the major problems lie, advertising people just cannot bring themselves to discussing them openly and in depth.

I have no problem in giving them a full airing. And they affect all of us in so many ways, whether you happen to be consumer or a producer, an advertising or marketing specialist.

So let's get on with it.

CHAPTER FOUR

The Only Thing Wrong with that Slogan is that I Didn't Write It

Once a creative ad team has learned as much about the client's product as possible, then the tough job begins, because seldom does a Big Idea jump right out at you. You have to play with the concept before you get it right.

Most Big Ideas originate with that strange and lovable breed of advertising people called copywriters and art directors. From my experience, few of them work in the same way. Sometimes the copywriter will simply write down different ideas — pages and pages of them — until the right one, the right words leap off the page. It is like solving a brainteaser. You have to open your mind to all the possibilities. An art director may tinker with visual images, positioning the product or service in different trappings, different settings. The best results often come when the two disciplines work together, playing off one another.

Others of the breed will simply go away for two days and let the juices flow. Then one morning you are presented with — the Big Idea. They've simply let their creative imagination churn until Bingo, there it is.

That is why there is no school for creativity in advertising. It can't be taught. It must be instinctive. It is original thinking brought to bear on a single existing item placed under microscopic surveillance. It is focussing onto something tangible while, at the same time, letting the imagination range across a wide spectrum of associated images. It is control and letting yourself go, both operating simultaneously.

As often as not, the Big Idea consists of words put together to present a succinct idea, a thought that sums up the visceral benefits of the product quickly and easily. Other times it is a visual approach that strikes at the heart of what you want to say. Or it can be a combination of both.

What you are always looking for, of course, is that unique way of summing up your product succinctly, dramatically, artistically. Only when you have incorporated these ingredients in your concept do you achieve the ultimate in good marketing: memorability. It is the vital bridge to consumer commitment. It provides the essential stepping stone when each of us makes a decision to buy.

But what constitutes a truly memorable Big Idea? That's a most difficult question to answer because, as one associate, Harrison Yates, put it: "it's either there or it isn't," which is a big help. Yet he's right in a way. Most of the time, it is obvious when you see it. Just as often it is almost impossible to explain. It can be in the salient feature of the product or service itself. It can be something totally unrelated. It can be a play on words. It can be a catchy, witty phrase. It can be visual impact. And it can be many, many other things as well.

Let's briefly look at some of the more memorable Canadian Big Ideas, then delve a little more deeply into four that I've been privileged to be associated with:

• Bell Canada's "The Long Distance Feeling". That phrase gave McKim Advertising the umbrella to get across the telephone giant's message in truly human terms. Simple, but effective. It associated the telephone with feelings of warmth, happiness, celebration. You just wanted to make a long distance call to friends or relatives. It wasn't lifestyle, it was purposeful. And there is a big difference between the two.

• "Only in Canada. . . . Pity." This brilliant line, which has served Red Rose so well for so many years, was developed by J. Walter Thompson. A classic, off-the-wall approach that could only have originated from the fact that the English are the world's greatest tea drinkers. Add the humour of their wonderful, colourful speech idiosyncracies and you have a Big Idea that is truly memorable. The ads say so much about the product's perceived qualities — without boring you.

• "Mainly Because of the Meat." It is from MacLaren, and it allowed Dominion Stores to position itself uniquely in juxtaposition to the other supermarkets. Everybody came to know what Dominion Stores stood for. It became a logical reason to shop there. After all, meat is generally the key item on your grocery list.

• "Our Product is Steel. Our Strength is People." The only thing wrong with that line is that I didn't write it. It's a superb corporate identity for Dofasco, developed by Russell T. Kelly. And still going strong. In fact, I doubt they'll ever drop it. It's timeless. It says it all.

• "Dare To Be a Priest Like Me." This concept was used exclusively on billboards to recruit seminarians for the Roman Catholic Archdiocese of Toronto. Now that is gutsy for a church. And it sure grabbed everybody's attention. It was created by Martin Keen, one of the special talents in Canadian advertising with whom I have the pleasure of working from time to time.

• "Super, Natural." Again by McKim, this time for the B.C. Ministry of Tourism. How simple, yet how graphic. A play on a word you would never expect to see in ad copy, let alone in a tourist campaign.

And, finally:

• "Will That Be Cash or Chargex?" It was developed for Visa out of McCann-Erickson. This one says it all, too. And just think of this for a moment. What do your competitors do to fight it when you have positioned yourself so well? You've boxed them out. They hate you.

None of these were accomplished easily. Yet all are so memorable. What corporation anywhere in the world, for instance, wouldn't like the rights to the Dofasco identity. And it wasn't developed in Toronto, or New York, or London, England, but in the company's home town of Hamilton. Creativity is everywhere.

Now, you may argue that all of these Big Ideas are word concepts, not visual ones. Well, you're partially right. But only partially. If you peruse some of them again more closely, you'll see that the words are essentially a summation of visual or other impact. The phrase alone may mean everything, or it may mean nothing unless accompanied by other ingredients. "The Long Distance Feeling" is dependent upon strong visual presentation sensitively and lovingly filmed to truly get its point across. So is "Dare To Be A Priest Like Me" (the visual was a crucified-Christ figure hanging over a modern city, and the daring, startling image connected with the copy line). "Super, Natural" is simply the obvious conclusion to the pictorial presentation of the visual beauty and majesty of B.C. and "Only in Canada. . . . Pity" makes no sense unless it's preceded by an obviously English dialogue. It's difficult, therefore, to distinguish between whether the visual or the word concept came first, or which is more important. Unless, of course, you were there. But the casting for the commercials are impeccably well done.

As a classic illustration of visual impact alone, there's no better example than the late Alan Fleming's logo design for Canadian National Railways. While some critics called it a white worm — and worse — they missed the point entirely. Simplicity has always been the key to good design. There is nothing simpler than Alan's concept, nothing more graphic, more easily identifiable, more memorable. That is why it is a classic.

Alan showed me the design when it was in its formative stages. He wasn't showing it to me for my approval. It was just that he was so excited, so sure of himself. You could tangibly feel his enthusiasm. It was like someone finding the Holy Grail. He knew he was there. And he was right, of course. Our friend Mr. Slick would have loved his design. He had a phrase: "An artist has more than two eyes, that's a fact." That succinctly sums up Alan's achievement on behalf of CN.

And all creative teams must have that same commitment to dig, to passionately commit to feel deeply about the client and his or her product. It is the only route to the Big Idea.

In my more than thirty years in advertising, I have been involved in hundreds upon hundreds of creative concepts. Some of them were so good, in fact, that as soon as you saw them, you knew they were bang on. You knew intuitively that you had captured the product or service in the best way possible. And when it happens, you glow. There is nothing quite like it in the world. Well, maybe perhaps the Northern Lights on a clear, crisp night. Or winning a 6/49.

Other times, the Big Idea, at first, leaves you cold. You think your people are hallucinating. You look at it and it says nothing to you. Yet it turns out it really *is* a Big Idea. That feeling mainly comes when you haven't put yourself in the shoes of the audience the concept was intended for. Your creative people have, but you haven't.

When the Big Idea escapes you, all you can do is argue it out; let the creative people convince you of its credibility. That is not easy, especially when you are the boss. It requires a certain give-and-take that you don't find in many other businesses. Then, after you have come to some form of consensus — and you must reach one — all you have to do is convince the client that it is a Big Idea.

Domtar: Goodis, Goldberg, Soren

Burroughs Canada: The Jerry Goodis Agency

Let's take a moment to study four Goodis examples of the Big Idea. Each of these — among others of mine — is included in *Colombo's Canadian Quotations*. The reason I want to discuss them in detail is because I know them intimately. Therefore, I can give you an in-depth perspective on how and why each was developed. While they may be old (or is it aging?), they are as applicable today as when they were first designed. And that is the true stamp of good creativity.

ELMER'S GLUE

Elmer's Glue was a household adhesive; a good product, but pretty undramatic when you looked at it from a marketing point of view. At the time we got the account, it was a minor division of Borden Canada Ltd. and, as the client told us: "We don't have a hell of a lot of money to promote it, but we have to make the effort." What client doesn't say that? With Elmer's, however, we understood. The budget allocation wasn't large. So, what else is new?

Gerald Rae, the president, was the man we reported to at Borden's. Over the period of time we dealt with him, I found him to be a demanding taskmaster, but, in contrast to his tough business demeanor, one who would allow you lots of latitude when it came to creativity. He loved Big Ideas.

The Elmer assignment fell to long-time personal pal and associate, Oscar Ross, a quiet guy who was given to staring out the window when he was doing his creative thinking. A couple of days after Oscar took on the assignment, he walked into my office and plunked a piece of rough artwork on my desk. I looked at it, then I looked at him. "Are you pulling my leg?" I asked. "No" he replied.

The artwork was simple. There were only four words of copy. They were: "Quick! The Elmer's Glue." The background was stark white. One corner of what was obviously a sheet of paper was folded back as if it were peeling. The only color was that of the presumed billboard panelling the paper didn't cover.

It was a gorgeous visual expression of what the product was supposed to do: stick things to things. It was different all right; but it was so simple as to be practically non-existent. At least, that was my first impression.

"Where?" I asked. "Billboards" was the reply. "Billboards? Are you out of your mind? Rae will never buy that."

You see, until only a few years ago, outdoor advertising was considered strictly a backup medium. Here was my creative guy telling me his whole campaign was based on using billboards exclusively. But the more I looked at it, the more it began to fit into place. Rules, as that horrible cliché goes, are made to be broken. . . or at least ignored.

Yes, the client had a small budget. We could be selective in our placement of the ads: high-traffic areas close to hardware stores in certain cities. A lot of visibility. And, after all, our target audience was every adult who might use a household adhesive, and the hardware dealers who were trying to move Elmer off their shelves. Finally, I got up the nerve to show it to Gerald Rae. The first thing he asked was whether it would work. I told him I believed it would. He bought it.

It worked beautifully indeed. Elmer's Glue did start to move off the shelves. We even developed miniature billboards to market the product with hardware-chain personnel. Everybody got the picture immediately, so to speak.

The lesson is obvious. Simplicity works as long as it is creative. This was probably the most simple creative concept I had worked with until then. The message could be understood in the blink of an eye, which is essential for outdoor advertising. We didn't talk about the product benefits; we just showed what they were — graphically. We didn't even show a photo of the product, just registered the name.

It was a perfect example of copy and art working hand-in-glove to achieve instant recognition, impact, and memorability. I came to love that ad. And, in its way, it helped to expand the field of outdoor advertising to many other products and services. As veteran ad man and *Marketing* Magazine's creative critic Ted Wood said of the Elmer's ad in choosing his ten favourite campaigns over twenty-five years (1958-1983): "A brilliant use of an often maltreated medium."

SWISS CHALET
Unlike many other popular prepared-food chains, Swiss Chalet was developed in Canada. The first time I became associated with it, it had about six outlets in Ontario and Quebec. The company's positioning in the marketplace was a simple one: Excellent barbequed chicken at moderate prices in pleasant surroundings. We lost the business when Goodis, Goldberg, Soren merged with MacLaren. Four years later, soon after we founded The Jerry Goodis Agency Inc., Swiss Chalet came home to roost (pun intended). . . along with Harvey's, the folks who make your hamburger a beautiful thing. The man we reported to was a brilliant and delightful gentleman to work with. Bernard Syron, a lawyer no less, who is now the chief of Cara Foods, which later became the corporate arm for Swiss Chalet, Harvey's, Grand & Toy, and other retail and airline food enterprises.

Because Syron could pinpoint the objectives of the chain vividly and articulately, and describe equally well what he was doing to achieve them, we gained an invaluable insight into the business immediately. Many clients cannot do that for you because they are not quite sure what they want other than an increased volume of sales. They haven't sat down and looked at their product in depth, its audience, and its perceived benefits.

This professional insight helped the copywriters assigned to the account to zero in quickly on a concept for Swiss Chalet. Others might have tried to capitalize on the corporate name itself, which would have been a grievous error. While we all appreciate the Swiss as an industrious, thrifty, conservative people, relating those attributes to barbequed chicken would have stretched the imagination too far. The name was fine because it had good connotations but the advertising had to come from another angle.

Steward Hood, our uncommonly talented gifted director, concentrated on the chain's mandate and finally settled on: "Never So Good for So Little." That summed it all up because it was an excellent product that was economically priced. What helped us in coming to that conclusion — and that phrase — was the fact that we gorged ourselves with the product, and came to appreciate it. I'm still addicted.

And that, as I've said previously, is a major factor in developing any creative concept for a client. You have to know the product well and believe in it with a passion. You have to get into it. Then, more often than not, the creative will flow from that appreciation, that knowledge. And, in the case of Swiss Chalet, that enjoyment.

The words of the slogan also had a delightful rhythm to them. They rolled off the tongue. It gave Swiss Chalet an appealing, down-to-earth flavour, one that would hold it in good stead as it grew. And grow it did. Eventually, when there were more than fifty outlets, Bernie Syron brought in designer Don Watt to freshen up the Swiss Chalet image. (Watt is the graphic designer who helped to turn Loblaws around one-hundred-and-eighty degrees and make it one of Canada's leading supermarket chains.) For our client, he developed a new trademark and redesigned both the exterior and interior of the outlets to give them a bright and comfortable feel that was even more attractive to customers. He and his people were a joy to work with on the project.

Now, of course, Swiss Chalet, often in combination with Harvey's, is located right across the country and highly popular in the U.S. as well. It's a true — but, nowadays, far too rare — Canadian success story.

In our creative approach to this client we simply adopted the company's mandate and translated it into clear-cut language that summed up the product and its moderate price succinctly to the public. It was successful because it reached potential customers in a way that was sympathetic to their needs and promised them an experience they would enjoy. Swiss Chalet, on its part, was determined to fulfil that promise. It did.

And, by the way, we developed the Harvey's theme as well: "Harvey's Makes Your Hamburger a Beautiful Thing." But that's another story.

Harvey's: The Jerry Goodis Agency

CANADIAN NATIONAL EXHIBITION
Michael Warren had just moved from the position of head
of the Toronto Transit Commission to being interim chairman of the CNE when we were invited to pitch the account.
We knew Michael was a young, strong-willed, aggressive,
demanding manager. He told us he wanted a marketing
strategy to put some new life into what we all considered
to be an aging spinster, stumbling, hobbling, gasping to survive. An anachronism — but which the city of Toronto was
committed to revitalize.

I didn't know Michael well then. We sparred a lot, which
is normal, I expect, between two headstrong, egomaniacal
people. Over the years, though, we became close friends.
Later, I was associated with him when he headed up that
demanding monster, Canada Post. He performed miracles
there, despite persistent interference from first Liberal, and
then Conservative ministers responsible for the Crown Corporation.

One of our many wonderful art directors, Gray Abraham,
was asked to head up the creative team for the CNE. It was
a tough assignment. Everybody took the fair for granted. And
it was truly aging. What could we do to breathe new life into
it? It meant spending a lot of time at the Ex trying to figure
out a new approach. It meant talking to everyone connected
with it. And we had to do it at a time when it wasn't open.
We had to depend, to a large extent, on our own memories,
the nostalgia it represented to those of us who had
experienced it.

Three days before we were to make our presentation to
Michael and the board of directors, Gray presented me with
the overall concept. The key line was: "For 3 Bucks You're
Laughing."

I was in disagreement with the creative team. I thought
the phrase was too mundane, too common, too undignified.
As far as I was concerned, it was just simply a play on words.
And I especially didn't like the word "bucks". It was slang;
street talk. The creative team insisted I was wrong. They
argued that a hell of a lot of good, ordinary people and kids
went to the Ex. The phrase summed it up for them. It alluded
to the low entry price and what you would get for it. It could
be used with any visual depicting the various activities of
the CNE, from the midway to the horse show.

The internal discussion — perhaps battle is a better word — raged back and forth, and the three days dwindled down to presentation time. Everybody liked it but me. When push came to shove, consensus was what I always strived for within our ranks. The agency, however, didn't lose. The CNE board of directors approved the concept and we went to work. And the campaign worked too. Attendance rose dramatically.

What did it all prove? First, it pays to talk to your audience as directly as possible. If you do it well, they will hear your message loud and clear. Secondly, when you get a Big Idea that can be used in any number of ways in practically any medium, then you have got something special. And, finally, I learned Goodis is not infallible. But don't tell anybody.

HIRAM WALKER & SONS LTD.

We went after the Hiram Walker account when their original agency got into financial difficulties. I described our initial pitch in my earlier book. "First I wrote expressing a compellingly keen desire to meet them and talk about their business. . . . Then we sent over a baseball bat with a Canadian Club label silk-screened on it. The note said: 'We'll help you Club your competition.' We sent other messages as well, just as cornball. But the technique got us in the door, and we were awarded the account."

While we developed ad campaigns for most of Hiram Walker's products, i.e., Imperial, Special Old, Drambuie, and Kahlua, our main initiative was directed toward Canadian Club, the company's flagship brand of rye whiskey. At the time, Canadian Club was second to Seagram's V.O. in popularity. Walker's wanted to turn that around. It was almost a passion with Lorne Duguid, a former N.H.L. hockey player, who was the distillery's tough vice-president of marketing. We gave it top priority.

Doug Linton, now a partner in a good agency that employs a lot of Goodis' graduates, gave us the marketing edge we needed. The key was the fact that Canadian Club was sold in eighty-seven countries around the world. Now, the question was, how do you take advantage of that fact with customers in your home country? I suppose there are many answers to that question, but I liked Doug's best. Associating the worldwide distribution with the fact that, at the time,

Sketchley Cleaners billboards produced by Goodis &
Sharabura Inc.; writer Martin Keen

Canadians were not overly self-confident, not prone to blowing their own horn (Have we changed that much?), he and his team came up with a concept that juxtaposed fact with attitude! "Buy Canadian. The Rest of the World Does."

All we had to do was portray the product prominently in juxtaposition to the copy. And Doug backed up the statement with supporting facts. After all, if you are going to retain your credibility, you have to convince your audience. The subtext read: "Smooth and mellow Canadian Club is the world's lightest whiskey. And 'The Best in The House' in 87 Lands." Then we named all of them. The eventual result: Canadian Club overtook V.O. as the Number One rye in Canada.

What we had done for Hiram Walker was make Canadians a little more proud. And they obviously appreciated it. Were we playing on their emotions? Of course we were. But there is nothing wrong with that. Emotion is used every day to persuade. If it is honest and sincere, it will be accepted.

So there we have it. Four ad campaigns, four creative approaches. The simplicity of words and visual presentation that told people what Elmer's Glue could do. The down-to-earth, direct communication that informed people what the CNE was all about. The succinct summation of the perceived benefits of dining at Swiss Chalet. And the emotional pride one could establish for a Canadian product.

For any Big Idea to make its point in the competitive marketplace it must be presented with artistry, memorability, integrity, and truth. These campaigns had all those ingredients. That is why they were so successful. They were believable.

An irony that has occurred to me over the past few years is that, although creativity appears to be on the decline in advertising, it is becoming increasingly popular in other media. For instance, in bumper stickers: "If you can read this, you're too damn close." "Baby on board, husband in trunk." "As a matter of fact I do own the road." In T-shirts: "Age is not important unless you're a bottle of wine." "I make house calls." "It's been lovely but I have to scream now."

And on all kinds of buttons: "Yes. . . but not with you." "Obviate obfuscation." "I touch the future. I'm a teacher."

Wonderful stuff. And, like a great deal of humour, much of it originates in one person's highly tuned imagination. For example, the other day I saw a phrase scratched out in the dust on the back of a transport truck. It said "Drive or Talk. Hang up the phone." Now isn't that appropriate to our time?

Obviously, there are a lot of sharp, non-advertising copywriters out there. Too bad they're not in the business. And just as many potentially good art directors. Just look at some of the more memorable graffiti you've seen; vulgarity excluded, of course. There can be revolution only where there is conscience; witness the graffiti used during the French students' revolt in 1968.

Advertising needs all the help it can get creatively. If you are imaginative and inventive, apply. Then again, if you are too inventive, too imaginative, some agencies will balk.

"Pity."

CHAPTER FIVE

If You Haven't Got an Idea, Create a Jingle

The Good, the Bad, and the Ugly. I know it's the title of an early Clint Eastwood movie, but it serves equally well as a graphic description of the present state of the art of creativity in advertising. Or, perhaps it would be more appropriate to reverse it because, to my mind, there are now more ugly ads than there are bad ones and definitely more ugly and bad than good. And "good" spans the whole spectrum from competence to excellence.

I'm not talking about the production side of advertising. In most cases, it is first-rate. Then again, it should be with all the filming, sound, and reproductive advances made available to the industry in the '80s. That, however, is a major part of the problem. As often as not, technique has displaced content. The Big Production has superseded the Big Idea. And big ideas have always been the foundation of excellence in my profession.

As I've always drummed into the people in my agency: "Second-rate execution of a first-class idea is far better than first-rate execution of a second-class idea." In other words, execution cannot save tired, threadbare ideas. It can only give them a faltering crutch upon which to lean. How many clothing ads have you seen with claylike male or female models posing as if they were sent down to us from the Mount with just the sponsor's name on it. . . Ralph Lauren or Yves St. Laurent. Then you have the Big Idea Levi's billboards where word and picture spark one another to deliver a sales message to us with elan and personality. Watch for the Levi's billboards and you will see — and watch for the former: tired, time-worn "get the photographer to take a great shot" billboards or magazine ads that are empty, vacuous.

The obverse of my creative beliefs appears to be more in vogue with present-day practitioners. It is as if they were brought up on the old adage: "If you pile enough of it against the wall, some of it's bound to stick. But, even if it does, it's still chaff." And chaff just won't do it. It's the lazy way to collect your fifteen per cent commission by doing as little creatively as possible. And it cheats your client.

Creativity is the essence of good advertising for the simple, but profound reason, that your ultimate task in any ad is to let people know about your product or service in a convincing, truthful, compelling manner and to do it with freshness and elan, just like the Milk Board commercials. The Milk Board commercials produced by McKim Advertising are wonderful because they employ very refreshing animation techniques and the spots are based upon real-life, human experiences. Life in today's maelstrom environment is tough, and energy-consuming for all of us, and a milk break can be not only health-giving but energizing and refreshing. They do not beat you over the head with unprovable claims, they do not boast, they don't overstate. They simply tell the truth in a charming and artistically breakthrough way. Technology can help you to achieve that, but it is no substitute for an original, creative idea. No way. Nowhere. No how.

What is so incongruous about so much advertising today is that it has become more dependent upon technical tricks and flash than upon product benefits, and it is doing it at a time when the consumer is becoming more knowledgeable, more selective, and needs to be talked to more thoughtfully than ever before. Adolescents of whatever age can always be conned into buying something at least once; but they are becoming scarcer as people become more sophisticated, more choosey about how and why they want to spend their hard-earned dollars. The shell game of technical wizardry just isn't good enough to create the required appeal. Or, if it does initially, it cannot sustain it.

Instead we have the ludicrous situation of ad agencies substituting for creativity with hype and excess. But hyperbolic ads are only confusing. And excessiveness is nothing but boring. Is that really what advertising is supposed to be about? To confuse? To bore? Of course not, yet that is what so many ads do nowadays. And all you want to do when you see or hear them is scream: "Please, no more!"

Retailers, especially auto dealers, furniture and discount stores, appear to be among the worst offenders. Leon's and The Brick to name two. A so-called spokesperson blabbers incessantly about "No money down." "No payments." "Don't pay a cent event." "Just walk right in and grab what you want." "Best prices in town." Three hundred words of script crammed into thirty or sixty seconds. Inventory sale! End-of-year sale! The last great sale! The first great sale! They have more sales per year than Heinz has brands. It reminds me of the old — and silly — joke about lay-away plans. "Only a dollar down and a dollar a day — 'till they lay you away." Poor marketing. Such a waste, and so damned insulting to the viewer.

To make matters worse, often ad agencies insult people's intelligence even more by placing identical spots in piggy-back style, one humped onto the other in a desperate effort to gain impact. That is nothing more than brainwashing consumers. No wonder advertising has such a tarnished image. No wonder someone invented the zapper!

In other words, more hype, repetition, and greater frequency are being employed to wear down you and me. More often than not, if you have a modicum of intelligence, you will ignore or zap such campaigns. They are not only boring and confusing, they are ugly.

On the other hand, when a good Big Idea comes along, we heed it in the same way we reject a bad idea. A Big Idea grabs our attention and holds it until it can make its point. If the proposition is worthwhile, then we will act on it. If not, it is probably because the product is something we don't need or want. But the key to any Big Idea is to gain and hold attention, not in a frenetic way, but in a thought-provoking one. Levi's, Buckley's, Bell's long-distance stuff are examples of fresh, thoughtful, clever, passionate ideas beautifully executed. They all get fair hearings because they treat the viewers as intellectual equals.

The Levi's campaign produced by Harrod & Merlin is graphically arresting and takes advantage of an oft-used technique in advertising — playing the words off the picture. One example is a photograph of a shapely girl's posterior with the Levi's jeans so tight on her body that the denim has actually split. The headline is "Split Ends", a rather obvious but

Split

Levi's: billboard produced by Harrod & Merlin

nevertheless amusing play on words and pictures. The implication is, of course, that there is nothing that will stop her from wearing her beloved Levi's even if, through prolonged wear, they are starting to rip.

Buckley's Mixture takes advantage of a disadvantage. The stuff tastes awful and the advertiser has the guts to say so. It is the truth. It is disarming. And it is executed visually and graphically in a superb manner by Doug Linton's agency.

In advertising, because it is constantly bamboozling the viewer with hyperbole, it is almost sacrilegious to tell the truth; but Mr. Buckley and the Linton gang have readily admitted that their product tastes terrible.

The Bell Telephone commercials take real-life situations (like children telephoning grandmother or grandfather) and with delicate and sensitive camera work and impeccable acting, simply remind us that it is good to stay in touch with

67

"I came by my bad taste honestly. I inherited it from my father."

Fortunately, Buckley's Mixture works on coughs and bronchitis just the way it worked when my dad invented it back in 1919. Unfortunately, it also tastes just the way it tasted back in 1919. Just remember what dad always said: "If it didn't taste the way it tastes, it wouldn't work the way it works."

It's how Canadians fight coughs.

"The good news is you don't have to drink it."

Just rub it on your chest. White Rub quickly loosens congestion caused by colds, and bronchitis. Dad never wasted time on a remedy that did anything but work hard. He was pleasantly surprised when he came up with White Rub. "I got lucky on this one," he said. "It feels good. And it works."

Buckley's transit cards: agency — Ambrose Carr Linton Kelly Inc.; reproduced with permission of Frank C. Buckley & John Meehan

those we love. The camera work, the casting, and direction of those spots are works of art. They are refreshing to the eye and to the ear when you compare them with what surrounds them: mouthwash commercials, automotive, retail furniture store commercials, and women's hygiene products (which, by the way, I think should be outlawed).

What more can the advertiser ask from an ad campaign than a fair hearing? That is why the Big Idea is so crucial to success.

Loblaws President's Choice and G.R.E.E.N. product are what I call a "Big Idea". Both young and old, world-wide, in ever-increasing numbers are becoming more and more concerned about environmental issues. Therefore, when you offer the consumer a range of products that are sound environmentally, you are bound to capture their attention. And, if your presentation of the product line is convincing, you are equally bound to win a significant percentage of them as customers to the detriment of other products that cannot compete on the same basis.

It was no accident that Loblaws was one of the first to move in this direction. Nor was it an accident that it named its products "Green". It was a defined marketing strategy to seek out such a range of products and to capitalize on it through the positive image the word "green" conjures up, which doubtless partly explains its presence in such organizational titles as Greenpeace and the Green Party, et al. I have noted with interest that the federal government is now getting on the bandwagon with its "EcoLogo" symbol, a maple leaf formed by three birds. In mid-March 1990, the first ten products were given the environmental seal of approval so they could use the logo. Whether it will work depends ultimately on what publicity support Ottawa gives to the program; although often government approval of anything contributes eventually to its demise.

Now, if one is jaded enough about the world, I suppose you could say Loblaws should not be cashing in on such a serious issue. I don't buy that. Loblaws is in the business of marketing as best it can against its competitors. If it can do that by finding products that present a definable, positive benefit, why should it hide such a fact from potential buyers? After all, what it did was nothing more than consciously respond to growing public concern and inform people what it was doing about it.

That is commendable. It is also good business. It's the same as responding to a health-conscious public with products that are sugar-free, salt-free, or calorie-reduced. On the other hand, I have serious problems with the tobacco companies continuing to advertise cigarettes as if they made you more socially acceptable when the opposite is the truth. That is gross, indecent, immoral marketing. The whole raison d'être is to show smoking in the most attractive light possible. And that, dear reader, is insidious marketing. It's a Big Idea all right; a BIG BAD IDEA.

The point I wish to make here is that the "Big Idea" is — and always has been — the focal point of excellence in marketing, promoting, and advertising goods or services. If you don't have one, then the producers of such products and services had best save their money. Unless, of course, they want to invent a fictitious benefit. Big Ideas do not come easily. Perhaps that is why they appear to be so unpopular among today's advertising gurus. All products and services have a unique personality. If they didn't, there would be no reason for them to exist. That is axiomatic. But a unique personality is different from uniqueness itself. Take, for instance, salt. All salt is essentially the same. If, however, you package salt so that it pours more easily, then you have a unique personality. It is not in the product, but in the packaging.

For many years this search for a product's personality was referred to in the profession as looking for its USP: its "Unique Selling Proposition". The phrase was invented by a famous American advertising man, Rosser Reeves. It has now gone out of fashion, mainly, I believe, because it was overly glib and too narrow a concept. It was open to too much ill-conceived interpretation. Be that as it may, it is still an essential guideline in helping to define a product's personality. And from that personality, to developing the Big Idea.

In order to accomplish this, any ad agency must become imbued with the client's product. You must know as much about it as if you were a long-time employee. You must witness it being manufactured and understand what it consists of. You must know why it was developed in one way and not another. You must know how it is priced and why. You must know its advantages over other products it is competing against, and you must know the target audience for which it was developed. Like an actor or actress, you have to live the role before you can play the part successfully.

After you have done all that, if you cannot discover a distinct personality, then you are in deep trouble. That, however, doesn't happen often for the simple reason that the vast majority of products and services are designed to fulfill a need in one way or another. On the other hand, too much contemporary advertising approaches the challenge from a perspective that has many pitfalls. Too often it simply forces a personality onto the product. It invents situations which it believes its prospective customers will relate to, then thrusts the product into the scenario. In other words, it invents a role and expects the product to play its part. That is like asking Danny DeVito to play Tom Cruise, or Roseanne Barr to play Michelle Pfeiffer. It doesn't work unless you want people to simply laugh at you.

It is called lifestyle advertising. An example: a housewife is trying to manage her home with small children and pets making a continual mess. Mr. Clean, Fantastik, or whatever, appears and all her troubles vanish with a quick swish of a cloth. Sometimes the product cleans all by itself; just spray away. Balderdash! It is never that simple; and, during such commercials, little or nothing is said about any of the perceived benefits of the product. The advertiser is depending upon perception through association.

Another example: London Life's "Freedom 55" campaign. You have young people transported to romantic, up-scale settings where they meet themselves twenty-five or thirty years down the road. "How can we afford all this?" is invariably the question. "London Life's Freedom 55" is just as invariably the answer. But what the hell is it? Is it participating life insurance? Is it a mutual fund, an RRSP? Or is it hocus-pocus? Who knows? The sumptuous lifestyle of the older "You" should be enough for the younger "You" to sign up right now. Or perhaps cost versus benefits has to be pointed out to you by a hard-driving salesperson sitting at your dining room table.

Sam Slick was wont to say: "Braggin' is advertisin'." And he was right. But you have to brag about something that is there, not simply intimate it is there; or worse, hope it is there. Perhaps modern advertising has simply adopted another Sam saying and placed a new, diabolical interpretation on it. That one goes: "To bung up a man's eyes ain't the way to enlighten him."

Now the rejoinder to all that I have said until now is that modern advertising must work, or why would advertisers spend so much money on it? Much of it is to maintain product loyalty by keeping the brand name continuously in front of the public. This is especially true if you are a leading brand. The top name in any line of products must sustain its image if it is to stay Number One. It is simply retention-marketing. Furthermore, one can assume that present users already respect the benefits in the product or service because they have continued to buy it.

But you do not simply dismiss the original Big Idea just because it is recognizable. That's silly. What you do is play with it, elaborate on it, give it a new vitality. After all, what got you there should be good enough to keep you there. A real problem, however, arises when a secondary brand — or brands — has the audacity to improve its product in a substantial way. The leader cannot ignore such an intrusion into its territory. It must react, and it can do so in a number of ways.

First, it can improve its own product. Indeed, it is far better to continually keep improving the product, no matter what the competition is doing. Mainly that is not done because such improvements can be costly and cut into profit margins. Therefore, often one just keeps doing the same old thing until you are challenged. But once a challenge is put forth, then all hell breaks loose. Take, for instance, the famous cola battles between Coke and Pepsi. It has been a tug-of-war for years now, each side plotting the demise of the other. Both have gone about as far as they can go. They may have even depleted the warehouse of Big Ideas, at least until they develop a new product, or a new wrinkle (Classic Coke, with its return to the original formula, barely made it). Now they seem to have settled into a long-term price war, especially in the supermarkets. Each week, one or the other is on sale — and highly promoted. It gives the impression that most of the public cannot tell one from the other; or they are just as happy drinking either. If that is the case, a lot of rethinking will have to be done to reposition either of them.

The problem with much brand improvement is that many products can only take so much of it. They get to a point where it is either uneconomical to improve, or the additional benefit is so inconsequential that it makes little or no difference. But, if you are really desperate enough, you will come up with something like "New and Improved". (By the way, most marketers don't like the word "new" alone because it connotes the negative impression that the product is untested or untried. Combine it with the word "improved", however, and they think you get a more positive image.)

Another alternative to a market challenge is to introduce a new line of a similar product. In that way you hope to maintain, or even increase, your market share when sales of the two are combined. And that is probably less intimidating than conjuring up new benefits to an already existing line since it is probably non-threatening to your present customers and you can position the new line to attract customers away from your competitors. Cereals often fall into this category.

But can you keep on doing this forever? In certain areas of products, yes; in others, no. With automobiles, for example, the limits are almost non-existent because styling, size, and price are an integral part of the marketing.

With beer it is a little more difficult, although, Lord knows, the beer companies have tried hard enough. First, they introduced "light" beer with fewer calories, which was a perceived benefit for many consumers. Then they introduced American-made beer, which was purportedly a taste benefit, although, to my way of thinking, it only confused the market. Now they have added "dry" beer (higher alcoholic content, but no so-called aftertaste). Molson's, the first in the field with this new beer, reports it has captured an astounding four per cent of the market in less than a year. The Big Idea for Molson Dry is "The Evolution of Beer" which it may well be. We'll wait and see.

The trouble many packaged goods have — detergents, beauty products, breakfast cereals, snack foods — is that there is only so much you can do with them. How many little cleaning crystals, how much Vitamin E, how much oat bran, how many raisins can you add to each of them? Even when a new wrinkle is added, almost every competitor jumps on the same bandwagon within weeks. All that does is confuse the buying public. And, more often than not, the consumer just stays with what he or she is already happy with. Improvement marketing, unless there is a definable, unique benefit added to the product, is a waste of both time and effort. And it is costly as well. On the other hand, advertising agencies just love it because it increases budgets — and that means more money in their pockets.

In some instances, agencies may exert an undue influence on producers to develop new, similar products because their research purportedly tells them there is a segment of the population they haven't reached yet, and is worthwhile going after. Maybe even a beer that would appeal to little old ladies. But anything is possible. The more I see of product-improvement advertising, the more I believe that unnecessary products and services are being forced onto the market to fill a gap that does not exist.

But when I see small companies simultaneously begin to take on the giants and their product lines, then I have to look twice at the original ones — and ask questions about whether they are truly satisfying consumer demand. Small companies are making inroads with preserves, snack foods — and beer. In the past few years, numerous small breweries have opened their doors, marketing beers that they say are more natural, and have more body and a better taste. Names like Upper Canada, Drummond, and Creemore — albeit sold regionally — are gaining on the big breweries. Reportedly, Drummond has ten per cent of the Alberta market. That is a dent in any market. (Some of them, unhappily, are closing their doors because of the current recession. . . .)

And there is a far greater choice now among preserves and condiments than there was a few years ago. Catherine's ("handmade with care"), of Toronto, offers such products as chili sauce, port jelly, and antipasto. Prince Edward Island Preserves, out of Charlottetown, produces, among other products, lemon and ginger marmalade, blueberry and raspberry jam with champagne. Even the potato chip giants are being nibbled at: Kettle Chips (with no preservatives), made by Lifestream Natural Foods in B.C.; Olde Barrel, out of P.E.I. (I know the P.E.I. Olde Barrel firm well. It is a co-operative venture of Acadian French P.E.I. farmers. I helped them design a new line of packages and posters which are hitting their marketplace as this book is going to press.) with its low-cholesterol, oat-bran chip, and Miss Vickie's, which are made in the village of New Lowell, Ontario, just down the road from the local beermakers in Creemore. One of the offshoots of this assault by smaller companies is that Hostess has now introduced Gibney's Chips, homestyle-cooked in sunflower oil. Delicious.

It proves that competition in the marketplace can be good for the consumer; much better, needless to say, than new and improved packaging.

Many of these products have succeeded with a single marketing strategy — natural quality. They boast having no ingredients in them with names you can't pronounce, or even know what they mean. Monosodium glutamate, which is a favourite. BHA, whatever the hell that is. Bacterial cultures, which send traces of fear through me. Hydrolyzed plant proteins, although this has two words that I can at least grasp. And polysorbate 80, a great title for a science fiction thriller. Government monitoring allows all of these ingredients to be added to products like ice cream, potato chips, soup, and frozen entrees so one assumes they are non-threatening. At the same time, most of us have no idea what they are, or even what they do. I do know one thing. None of them has a unique selling proposition. None of them gives me an inkling of a Big Idea.

As a marketing man, however, I do know that, if somebody comes to me and says: "Our product only has pure, unadulterated ingredients," then my eyes light up and I respond: "There is a market for that. It may not be large at present, but it is growing. And customers have no problem paying more because they want what they perceive as good, old-fashioned quality." And Catherine's — with no preservatives added — can inform you that their products have a shelf life of one and a half years unopened, two months in your refrigerator once opened.

Perhaps this is the true raison d'être for much lifestyle, product marketing. If you want it quick and easy, we will give it to you that way but you will have to get BHA with it, although we have no intention of mentioning the fact. We will just show someone lapping it up in a setting you will relate to. On the other hand, if you want homemade quality, then we will convince you to buy it with homemade quality.

Now that's a Big Idea!

CHAPTER
SIX

McLuhan's Media —
And Mine

"The medium is the message." That ringing phrase made the late Marshall McLuhan famous. He had his disciples, of course, and his critics. I admit I was somewhere in between, agreeing with much of what he said about modern mass marketing, disagreeing with his glib, and often banal, portrayals of the profession, and not quite understanding his theories when they extended beyond my own field. (I ain't so intellectual. . . .)

I could easily follow *The Mechanical Bride*, his first book, published in 1951. I didn't necessarily like what I read, but I understood him. Even appreciated his insight — sometimes even his wit. The interesting offshoot of that book was that, although he lambasted advertising and the media in a biting way, it made him the darling of the profession, especially along Madison Avenue. The consummate irony came with the publication of *Understanding Media* in 1964. The industry went a step further. Instead of being incensed at his theory that ads were being developed almost exclusively as a mosaic of status imagery to enhance demand for a product (in simpler terms, lifestyle advertising), it only intensified efforts to capitalize on that process. My, it is a wonderful business we work in.

McLuhan's preface to *The Mechanical Bride* opened on this note: "Ours is the first age in which thousands of the best-trained individual minds have made it a full-time business to get inside the collective public mind. To get inside in order to manipulate, exploit, control is the object now. And to generate heat not light is the intention." Thousands of the best-trained individual minds, my foot. This was the late '40s, remember. A few of them might have been college educated, but most gravitated to advertising because they felt at home in its non-conformist world, with its even more benign lifestyle, especially in creative departments. McLuhan made it sound as if they were involved in an evil, world-wide master plan you would find in a James Bond movie.

If you substitute the words influence, challenge, and persuade for manipulate, exploit, and control — each of which can be, more or less, synonymous with its corresponding word — then you have simply another definition of advertising. His words simply have a more sinister tinge: the castigating depiction of the ad man as propagandist and evil genius. But that is laughable. As well, good advertising requires light in order to generate heat. All by itself, heat just does not work unless it deals with a highly emotional issue. I can only agree with his conclusion if he was talking about truly bad advertising — not *all* advertising.

In his *Mechanical Bride* essay on automobile ads, he noted that much of what was said about cars in them could also be said about women. In other words, when men were the main purchasers of automobiles, copywriters linked male desires subliminally to generate impact. Cars and women had similar sex appeal. Or, as McLuhan put it in his flippant manner: "Hitch sales curves to sex curves."

Perhaps he was right. Then again, maybe he was just reading too much between the lines. Many young ad people then were swayed by the highly emotional advertising associated with World War II. Most of them had grown up with the good-guy-bad-guy images and the win-at-all-cost rhetoric of the war. And subliminal symbolism was the way of the art world. They were obviously very much a part of McLuhan's world. The way models dressed, the kind of automobiles they posed with, the famous Marlboro cigarette tattoos on macho cowboys, background music in commercials, were all considered to be subliminal mirrors of how we citizens dreamed of our rightful places in society.

More sensible and convincing, however, is the conclusion that such copywriting just came naturally as competition for attention in ads increased. And, if the car was considered a sex symbol to the male, why not compare it to a woman?

The art of fine tailoring lives on.

Ashbridge
BY SUSSEX

Ashbridge
BY SUSSEX

***Ashbridge Clothes — writer & art director Gerry Cooper —
The Jerry Goodis Agency***

Perhaps McLuhan simply opened a Pandora's box with his theories, one that elevated ad people to a level they never knew existed. They certainly embraced much of what he said — and began thinking his way. Does that make him unconsciously Machiavellian? Or am I beginning to think like him? Later, as TV became "The Medium", McLuhan would extend his insight to it as well. "The trend in ads is away from the consumer picture of product to the producer image of process" he wrote in *Understanding Media*. That is again an erudite way of describing what I call lifestyle advertising.

I agree with him when he says "Ads seem to work on the advanced principle that a small pellet or pattern in a noisy, redundant barrage of repetition will gradually assert itself. Ads push the principle of noise all the way to the plateau of persuasion. They are quite in accord with the procedures of brain-washing." But, in the beginning, was it planned, or was it just the obvious way to produce television ads, mirroring the themes and scripts of regular television programming? I am inclined to think the latter is true. At the same time, if I wanted to be devious, I could twist and contort McLuhan's phrase "The Medium is the Message," but that would be manipulative, even exploitive. I do not want to do that. I do believe, however, that the message has to be conducive to the medium it appears in. Therefore, in Goodis' terms, the medium *dictates* the message.

Your creative application of a Big Idea has to be adapted to the various media you will be using. Indeed, the creative approach may almost demand you use a specific medium. Take, for example, "Quick, The Elmer's Glue." Its impact was far greater on billboards than it would be anywhere else. Nike footwear, Porsche automobiles, Canada Post billboards would not work as well on radio, or in newspapers.

For centuries the dominant medium was print. It is also one of the most difficult to work with because, especially in newspapers, there is so much competition for the reader's attention. And it is not just the various ads that may be situated on the same page. It is the news itself. Rape. Gulf War. GST.

If you are intrigued by a news headline, and you become engrossed in the article, are you really going to pay attention to the ad adjacent to it? Probably not. If a photo grabs you, and you must read the outline, will you become oblivious to the advertising messages on the same page? Probably yes. In order to overcome such inherent — and natural — distractions, newspaper advertising has to drive home its message as poignantly as it can. The headline often holds the key to achievement. It has to be bold, expressive, eye-catching. If you use a photograph or illustration, it must triumph over the accompanying photo-journalism.

Most often the greatest success comes from a combination of verbal and visual impact. Ever since the introduction of lithography, we have been attuned to taking in both the

GOOD NEWS FROM (ARE YOU READY FOR THIS?) THE POST OFFICE.

There's a whole new life at the Canada Post Corporation.

Believe it or not, things have gotten better in the last little while.

Fact. During the first quarter of 1982, 83% of all first class mail was delivered on time, compared to 74% for the same period of 1981.

This is a definite improvement. But if you're still part of those who got a late letter or cheque, we admit that you still have every right to expect more.

And it will happen. The improvement mentioned here is but one that can be found in our newly instituted quarterly report which charts for you—our customers—our progress and improvement.

(You can get it by writing "Report", Canada Post Corporation, Ottawa, Ontario K1A 1H1.)

Furthermore if next quarter, things aren't as good, we'll tell you that too, because we know it's not all going to happen overnight — but it is going to happen.

You see, all possible improvements take their origins from our total dedication to better service. Which is our main commitment to the Canadian Public.

Which is why we initially set up a program of "Quick Starts" under some of our best managers who were told to immediately attack six critical areas in the processing and delivery of mail.

Then we initiated a special body called The Service Improvement Group—charged with the responsibility of seeing that progress continues on schedule.

The results to date are gratifying. We can feel it throughout the entire Corporation and we hope you'll start to notice too.

Thank you for your attention.

THE CANADA POST CORPORATION. IT'S STARTING NOW. AND IT'S GOING TO HAPPEN.

Canadä

Canada Post — The Jerry Goodis Agency

picture and the caption at the same time. One without the other is seldom satisfying. There must, however, be a linkage. Perhaps more to the point, a spark must be ignited between them. They must play off one another in order to gain the reader's attention. One example, taken when *Time* magazine set aside space to inform its readers about witty headlines and captions, showed a photo of the late Princess Grace of Monaco, admiring flowers in her garden. The caption was: "Monaco forecast, a little Ranier in February." The two elements played off one another to inform the reader she was expecting her first child by her husband, Prince Ranier. Corny? Yes. It was also memorable. And it entertained at the same time.

What you certainly do not want to do in print advertising is to be obvious. You don't want to show a picture of an outhouse and have the headline say: "This is an outhouse." That insults the reader because what it really says is: "See, stupid, this is an outhouse." Nor do you do things just to be provocative. You do not show a man hanging upside down just for effect. People will know you are simply employing a gimmick to gain their attention. But you might use an upside-down man if the point of your ad is that coins or keys cannot fall out of his pant pockets, no matter what position he is in. The headline, however, would have to capture that thought so readers know they aren't being tricked. (Bill Bernbach, my mentor, taught me that).

One of the better ways of achieving an effective linkage between copy and illustration is called the juxtaposition of opposites. Marshall McLuhan said it succinctly: "There can be a symbolic unity among the most diverse and externally unconnected facts or situations." For instance, I've just co-ordinated an ad campaign for the Koffler family's King Ranch, a new health spa north of Toronto. In one of the print ads the photo shows a woman, draped with a towel, sitting in a fetal position. It is a beautifully composed photograph. And what does the headline say? "The most powerful force on earth is the mind and body working together." That ad will stand out in any print setting. Why? Because there's a linkage between the headline and the photo, pulling in the reader. It's a subtle juxtaposition of opposites that arouses your attention. The illustration could be for any product or service, not necessarily a health spa. On the other hand, the headline

Canada Brick — Goodis & Sharabura Inc.

makes a statement you're not expecting. In fact, the strength of the statement is enhanced by the simplicity of the photo. And the photo takes on new meaning because of the headline. That ad, by the way, was the work of writer Norman Lehman.

Effective creativity in print advertising is not easily come by, and it is not simply a function of size. Naturally, size may help. If you take a full page ad, you have the potential to gain more attention than if you buy a small, one-column box. But the excitement in the ad must be there. Obviously, budget restrictions do not allow all advertisers to purchase full pages or double trucks (two facing-page ads). Needless to say, then, as much creativity has to go into the small ad as into the big one. It does not always require a Big Idea: maybe even just a little one that gives you Big Exposure.

I recently saw an ad in the Collingwood (Ontario) *Enterprise Bulletin* for a local store called Squire John's. It was advertising patio furniture and barbeques. It was a relatively small ad (two columns by seven inches), but it had the required impact because the headline read: "Are you play-ing with a full deck?" The remainder of the ad showed a deck setting and the names of the corporate lines carried by the store.

In magazine advertising, the problem is not as formida-ble since the format is smaller and the battle for attention less frantic. Still, most magazine ads also depend on strong headlines and graphic illustrations. The potential of excel-lent reproductive colour is an added bonus.

Because of the restrictive elements and the unique challenges of print advertising, it is becoming more and more a specialty field for agencies which limit their work almost exclusively to local and regional retail marketing. And a num-ber of large agencies have themselves set up retail divisions, separate from their main interests. That is how specialized it has become. Although print advertising is obviously less glamorous than writing and producing TV ads, the creative teams must be just as experienced at copywriting and art. And it can be just as rewarding as big-budget TV marketing.

The guidelines may be narrower, the budget smaller; but the thinking must still be Big. Back in the sixties when youth was rebelling in the U.S., police officers often became sym-bols of contempt because of their unenviable job of control-ling demonstrations, and breaking them up when they got out of hand. A print ad was developed to defend the image of the police. What it said in stark, bold type was "Cop: Fuzz: Flatfoot: Pig: What do you call one when you need one?"

When a special TV program on Clint Eastwood was sched-uled for his hometown of Minneapolis, the ad agency obtained a photo of him as a child, dressed in a cowboy out-fit. The caption under it said, "Go ahead, make my lunch." Yes, you could say they were lucky to get the photo. But once having obtained it, they did the most they could with it. I suspect no one who saw that ad forgot it — or the program it was advertising.

One major advantage of print advertising is that it is not as ephemeral as most other media. In radio and television, the message is there one moment and gone the next. With print, you can always return to it as long as you haven't thrown the material out. You can study the ad in detail. You can cut it out and return to it at a more convenient time.

You can even discuss it within the household to get a consensus on the product advertised. That gives print advertisers a huge advantage. And it makes it doubly important that potential buyers see your ad in the first place.

Because so much print advertising is devoted to local and regional marketing, it demands subtly different approaches: what retail specialist Morris Saffer calls "Store Wars". Unlike national advertising, the vendor is not out to build or reinforce product identity over an extended period of time. Local retailers have to get action from their ads immediately. People have to come in and buy, or the advertising is ineffectual. Such motivation does not detract from the Big Idea; it just alters the emphasis you place on it.

There are two theories about retail advertising. The first says that you should always highlight product in your ads because that is what you are selling. The second is that you should develop a personality for your establishment because it builds long-term benefits. In the first, you look at product from the point of view of immediacy and volume purchasing; in the second you look at the retail establishment from the perspective of image and the wooing of regular customers.

I lean more to the personality theory. If the individual product (or products) depicted in your advertising doesn't interest consumers immediately, then they are going to tune you out. On the other hand, personality will register more lastingly with potential buyers because it is attuned to their overall needs and desires. And once they have been attracted to the store — and see its range of goods — they are far more likely to come back than if they just went there to make a one-time, single purchase.

All retailers go through good times and bad because of the cyclical nature of the economy. If you are strictly product oriented, your ads will have to change dramatically in a recessionary period in order to attract customers. Indeed, it seems to me that retailers, who stress product exclusively, dramatize price alone in a downturn. That can be construed as weakness. And, if everybody is doing it, how can you get the attention you so desperately need? If, however, you have developed a personality for your store — and a steady clientele — you are in less trouble in bad times because people are more conditioned to shop with you. Perhaps it is a subtle point; but retailers must come to grips with it, even if it means a combination of both types of advertising. Indeed that may give you the best of both worlds. Numerous retail chains (at least until the introduction of the GST and the onslaught of the 1991 recession), Majestic, Loblaws, Burger King, and The Bay, for instance, stress personality in their TV ads, product in their print advertising or flyers, as does Shoppers Drug Mart. But that requires large budgets, which most stores do not obviously have. Nor does it matter what type of business you are in — low end or high end. Loyalty, I believe, is the way to success over the long run. And sustained image is the key to that loyalty.

The print media can be as powerful as television. It is not a second cousin, one that you use only when you cannot afford the more expensive one. To stress the point, the daily newspaper is the leading medium in ad revenues across Canada (and that is excluding the classifieds). Granted almost two-thirds of that volume is local advertising. But when you add in weekly newspapers and general-interest magazines, more than half of all advertising is in print. It is also a medium you do not dare abuse. Your advertising has to be as good in print as in any other vehicle if it is going to do the job.

Radio is a medium I love. Why? Because, as has been said so often, it is theatre of the mind. It presents a challenge unlike any other. On the radio, you don't have any visuals. Nor do you have headlines. The only potential tools you possess are voices, music, and sound effects. That is a challenge creatively — and perhaps one that is not clearly appreciated by a younger generation of copywriters who didn't grow up with radio as the sole electronic medium.

Before television, families used to gather around the radio and listen to programs other than simply music. Drama and comedy played a major role in their lives and attracted large audiences. In order to sustain the drama or to heighten the comedy, producers used the only elements they could — those you could hear. And they did it with great effect. The squeaky door that made you anticipate something eerie was about to happen. The sudden shriek that sent chills up and down your spine. The recognizable phrase or sound effect that identified a particular player or situation in a comedy routine. The dramatic pause before a punchline was delivered. It was all done to excite your imagination. Radio offered you a visual blank cheque, triggered by audio alone.

Today many ad agencies and creative teams don't understand the medium, although it is a highly popular advertising vehicle (about sixteen per cent of all ad placements). I am impatient with jingles that treat the audience as if it were pre-school children. I am depressed when I hear unfunny, high school humour being employed to try to convince you and me to make mature buying decisions. Have you seen the Black's Camera commercials, the Shoppers Drug Mart Christmas commercials or the old Leon's Furniture commercials which use one-line gags which the poor, hapless viewer is fed at least five times a night each? A bad joke told once is bad enough, but five times a night? Somebody please spare us. And I am shaken by the inept delivery of so many professional actors and actresses. Yet radio has enormous potential for those adroit and talented enough to use it wisely. In the hands of a professional copywriter and producer, it is a thirty-second play, a sixty-second symphony. In the hands of an amateur, it is a lethal weapon.

One of the classic skits developed for radio was Abbott and Costello's "Who's on First, What's on Second?" It was a magnificent play on words, incorporating misunderstanding, tension, frustration — all done to make us laugh uproariously for minutes on end. The writing was as skillful as you will ever find. The delivery was fast and furious. Later, when they performed it on television, little if anything was added to the performance. It didn't need visual impact to make its point. The skit, after many years, is still a bestseller on audio cassettes.

Today, the attitude toward the audience in many radio commercials is "You are not very bright. We know that. Therefore, we are going to sell you this product or service by coming down to your level. We are using a nursery school jingle so you can memorize the product's name. Or we will tell you a story using a wimpy wife or a weak husband. Or, perhaps, a joke that will be obvious to you because we'll give away the punchline."

Radio to be effective has to be stimulating. Furthermore, the inflection and the timing of the delivery must be impeccable. That is the only way to get the listener to pay attention to you. I would rather have commercials delivered by station announcers reading straight copy than an expensively produced spot that demeans its audience. At least in-house announcers are recognized and have believability working for them. They are friends of the audience. That is a better starting point than a script delivered with clanging cymbals and vacuous nonsense.

In radio, if you work at it diligently, you have everything going for you because, as I said before, the theatre resides in the mind of the listener. It is not a one-dimensional medium. You can make people see colour, taste flavour, feel passion and anger, and dream of places they want to be or things they wish to possess. The sound of a loon is distinctive to Canadians. If you employ that sound, there is no limit to the imagination it conjures up in each individual listening to it. What you have to do is relate it (but only if it is appropriate) to the item you are advertising. Then you have an attentive audience.

There are hordes of such symbols available to creative copywriters. Choosing the right one is the key to memorability. There are an almost equal number of voices that one can use, depending upon the inflection desired. The music can be rock, but it need not be. It can be an excerpt from a symphony or a sonata. Whatever is appropriate. Whatever makes your ad distinctive from the noise surrounding it.

In radio there are few restrictions and an almost infinite number of opportunities. It is truly theatre that your audience participates in. It is sound that translates into pictures in your head. It is voices that are warm and friendly, encouraging and convincing. Like print, radio is popular among retailers because its strength is local. And it has the added advantage of giving you increased frequency on a comparatively inexpensive budget. Because it is generally limited to the material you can get into a thirty-second or a sixty-second spot. It should be used more to build the personality of the advertiser than to sell a specific retail product. Television is an over-rated advertising medium. It is, of course, the big medium. It is second only in popularity among advertisers to daily newspapers. It carries just over fifty per cent of all national advertising (the dailies overtake it when local ads are taken into account). It is a billion-dollar business, not counting production costs.

But look at TV this way. What are the goods you see advertised mainly on television? Outside of such big-ticket items as cars, trucks, TV sets, furniture, and computers, most of the products marketed on the tube are items that you can buy individually for less than a five-dollar bill. Most of the products promoted on TV are related to finance, petroleum, cosmetics, health care products, fast food, beverages, and travel. These mainly emanate from large corporate entities with branches or outlets all across the country. TV is essentially the national advertiser's medium.

Let's look at who won the 1990 *Marketing* Magazine awards for excellence in single TV ads. The Gold went to Delsym cough syrup, the Silver to Oreo cookies, the Bronze to Black Label beer. The Certificate of Merit awards were: Labatt's Blue, Champagne cookies, Crunchie chocolate bars, Eggo waffles, Duracell batteries, Christie's cookies, Levi's jeans, the Volkswagen Corrado, Sanyo TV sets, Digital electronic equipment, Rubbermaid products, and Canadian Tire bicycles. Now all that should tell us something. What it tells me is that television is the medium of mass marketing, mass persuasion.

Yes, a significant percentage of TV ads is for packaged goods (items you can buy in any supermarket), fast foods, beer, and soft drinks. Media Measurement Services estimates that the four big spenders in Canada in each of these product categories (Procter & Gamble, Labatt's, McDonald's and Pepsi) budgeted almost $175,000,000 collectively on advertising in 1989. Four companies! And a significant proportion of that went to television. Procter & Gamble, to clinch the point, is the largest television advertiser, spending an estimated $50,000,000 of its total $60,000,000 on TV.

Yet TV accounts for barely thirty per cent of all net advertising revenue. Therefore, in many ways television is a vertical medium, only feasible for companies that produce products or services in vast quantities on a national or international basis.

In the advertising industry itself, television is larger than life because it means big budgets, big productions, big expense accounts, prestige, and all the rest of the pizzazz associated with the glamor of the business. When I meet people who are not in the profession, invariably their first question is: "What TV commercials have you produced lately?" They associate advertising with television. It's Hollywood, and they prefer it to Main Street.

Granted, ninety-nine per cent of Canadian households are equipped with TV. And fifty-six per cent of those have two or more sets. TV is big. No doubt about it. Everybody watches it, almost every day. Everybody talks about what they saw, or what they intend to see. Everybody knows the ads, whether they love them or hate them.

Yet television is also restrictive because it is the most expensive medium. A 30-second spot on either the full CBC or CTV networks can cost anywhere from three thousand to nearly twenty-five thousand dollars, the rate depending on the number of times it appears and when. The production costs on that same 30-second spot can range from twenty thousand up to a million dollars. I am not sure that for many advertisers the expense is worth it.

Once upon a time (which seems an appropriate phrase for the escapism of TV programming), the medium was the hottest thing in town. For many advertisers it still is. Now, however, with remote-control channel switching, VCRs and video rental stores popping up like mushrooms, and other options to regular programming, television must be re-assessed as an advertising medium. And many questions must be asked. Is your major audience children, adolescents, and retired people? Are they really the people you want to reach? Are news and sports becoming the major viewing preferences along with, perhaps, afternoon soap operas? Where, then, do you put your ad bucks to effectively reach your target audience? Is the public spending more of its leisure time (and reportedly that leisure time is dwindling, not increasing) doing things other than watching TV? Does TV advertising really reach people effectively?

Formerly, most TV commercials lasted sixty or thirty seconds. As costs increased, the 15-second spot became more and more popular. As that trend became more pervasive, friends began asking me if the networks and stations were being allowed more advertising time. Their perception was that, because there were more ads, more time was devoted to them. These people didn't realize that they were just seeing shorter ads. All they knew was that their space was being invaded more. And they didn't like it.

Most television advertising drives me up the wall. It is not because the production qualities lack excellence, but because the creative approach is too often just plain god-damned infantile.

Television advertising has an inherent social responsibility. In regular network programming, if you are talking about the rich and famous, we expect to see opulent settings. We have no problem with that. It is escapism. We may be somewhat envious, but we still lap it up. When you see an ad, though, that is promoting an inexpensive, everyday product, and the setting is a glamorous kitchen or a luxurious living room, what happens? What happens is that those viewers who aren't affluent become angry and resentful because the ad doesn't mirror them. They know it instinctively and they react automatically. I think they turn off the product. Nearly all of us have TV sets regardless of our financial status, but the less affluent probably watch more TV. Upscale ads are developed on the higher floors of an ad agency's headquarters by people wearing fashionable clothes and wondering about what fancy restaurant they'll have lunch in today. They reside not in the real world.

The advertising profession has an obligation to all, as well as to the client. This is especially so with TV. If you are advertising Club Med and you show sandy beaches, windsurfing and whatever, viewers will accept it, even if they don't have the money to go, because it's real. It's what Club Med is. And reality doesn't frighten most of us. If, on the other hand, you are promoting an anti-perspirant and the scene is a fancy-dress ball, those same viewers will tune you out. They know you are being snobbish. So they might very well snub your product because it is the only retaliation they have.

Obviously, TV ads should aim themselves at a targeted audience. McDonald's and Harvey's are good examples. Average people are seen. There are others, though, that do a disservice, not only to the profession and the client, but to our society. A graphic example: In a multi-racial country like Canada, you cannot continuously cast models or actors for TV roles who are white-skinned (or pinko-gray, which is closer to the truth). If you do, you discriminate against those of other colours — and they will undoubtedly discriminate against your products. Who can blame them?

Television is a tricky medium; one that I don't think my profession has yet come to grips with totally. It may be a glamorous medium, but it is also a sensitive one. It may produce huge audiences, but it is wasted unless a message is gotten across in a manner that is sympathetic, relevant, and

appealing to that audience. A TV reel in personal ad port-
folios may give creative people the illusion they are successful, but, unless they can work just as effectively in the other
media, they are little more than carney hucksters in a business where there are too many sleight-of-hand artists already.

Outdoor advertising is a bit of a misnomer because it
includes applications that are not strictly outside. Transit
advertising can be inside or outside public transportation,
and there are poster ads which can be located anywhere from
a bus shelter to a shopping mall. But outdoor advertising is
an excitingly creative medium; my favourite after radio. It
is obviously favoured by many other ad people too. If that
weren't the case, there wouldn't be as much stimulating,
original outdoor advertising as there is. Indeed, more good
creativity may have been developed for outdoor than any
other medium. It shows. A perfect example is the simple campaign developed by a branch of the outdoor business itself.
I've seen it in posters and on public benches. All it says is:
"You just proved poster advertising works." Now, talk about
your off-the-wall creative. The beauty of it, of course, is that,
if you don't see it, you don't know it exists; but, if you do,
the point has already been made.

I am not quite sure why so much outdoor advertising is
of such a high quality. Perhaps it is because it is so confined,
or because the rules of the game — creatively — are so few,
yet so precise. The main rule is that you only have a few
seconds to make an impression, register your product, and
tell your story. Depending on whether you are driving, walk-
ing, or a transit passenger, the time the advertiser has to register a product with you varies. Still it is frighteningly brief.
Maybe that demands it be frighteningly good as well.

The other rule is that the copy or the visual (or a combination of both) must be strong enough to make an impact
just as quickly. No ambiguity is allowed. No tedious disser-
tation is permitted. You have to get right to the heart. Perhaps because the rules are so precise, the concept must be
just as concise. Maybe creative people are simple-minded
individuals who are more at home with one small, delicate
mechanism than they are with a large, complex machine.
Maybe that is why the degree of excellence in outdoor far
outshines that in television advertising. One is concentrated
creativity, the other has a myriad number of intricate facets

CAN THEY AFFORD TO
SETTLE FOR ANYTHING LESS
THAN THE REAL McCOY?

Take a close look at the kind of people who
will buy new homes in the nineties. They're better
informed than ever before. And more and more, they
know exactly what they want.
They want value, quality, and choice. They
want The Real McCoy - genuine burned clay brick
by Canada Brick.
Nothing equals the value of burned clay
brick. No other material performs as well, over a
wider range of conditions - or looks as good while
doing it. And when it comes to choice, only
Canada Brick has such a complete range of colours,
textures and styles.
Fact is, when you tell them you're using The
Real McCoy, it says as much about you as about
the homes you build.
And like your customers, you can't afford to
settle for anything less.

416-821-8800
Call and ask for a sales representative.

"THE REAL McCOY" by Canada Brick

Canada Brick: Goodis & Sharabura Inc.

that may often convolute — and even defeat — an overall
concept. Be that as it may, outdoor advertising offers an amaz-
ingly wide spectrum of possibilities. It can be employed in
national or local campaigns; it can be a short-term blitz or
a long-term assault; it can be used broadly geographically or
selectively. It is a great medium.

Some will say that outdoor has proliferated in the land-
scape to such an extent that it takes away from the beauty
of natural surroundings. In some cases I agree. I don't want
to be driving along a scenic route and have a bunch of billboards break the spell. That is visual pollution. And, I admit,
in certain areas of our cities billboards are located inappropri-
ately. However, there are not as many as some people think.

On the positive side, billboards and posters can add verve
to the cityscape, especially if they are done with taste. They
are an attractive alternative to glass and concrete because
they are colourful and creatively interesting, which many
buildings certainly are not. They can provide a sparkle and
a witty focal point in juxtaposition to the grayness of the
streets and the traffic that fills them with a seemingly endless flow of cars. Incidentally, as of early 1990, Toronto's City
Council wants to ban taxis from carrying small poster adver-

tising on their roofs. Supposedly, council is worried about the visual pollution. I wish such councils would spend their time solving the other, more pressing problems in our cities, like housing for the poor. Furthermore, it is ludicrous to ban taxi ads when there is no intention of getting rid of similar ads on the sides and backs of public transit vehicles. Politicians!

The best posters and subway advertising for the past ten years have been produced in England, especially those which appear in the London underground. One that has been my favorite is sponsored by The Royal National Institute For The Deaf. On either side of the board are close-cut illustrations of a human ear. In the middle of the board the following copy appears: "Just Because We're Deaf, It Doesn't Mean We've Nothing Between Our Ears." Another one which I saw in the London subway is a beautiful full-color photograph of a mid-sized car driving through a rainstorm. But instead of tires it had nautical life-rings in their place. The implication by Dunlop Tyres is that Dunlop Tyres, especially in the rain (the photograph was taken on a dark and dreary night), are the safest thing you can have on your automobile in bad weather. The agency, Abbott, Mead, Vickers/SMS, is to be commended for that brilliant poster. The Institute For The Deaf poster was designed by Ogilvy & Mather. Saatchi & Saatchi did a stunning election poster for Margaret Thatcher's Conservatives during their last election which I happened to see in London as well. On the far right-hand side of the poster there was an illustration of a British marine with his arms upstretched in the "I Surrender" position. The headline read "Labour's Policy On Arms".

Not only is outdoor advertising succinct and creatively professional, but it's a personal medium, much akin to T-shirts and buttons that display simple, straightforward, often witty messages. And, if we are attuned to such graphic, individual expression, why can't businesses reach us in much the same manner? It is because billboard-style marketing has been so effective that many clothing manufacturers now emblazon corporate logos and product messages on the apparel they produce. They are memorable and make a simple, pointed statement.

The most powerful word in the English language is . . . SEX.

As has been often said, you could print that simple, three-letter word on almost anything — including a railway time-table — and people would be drawn to it, would even pay good money to buy a copy. In fact, it is probably the only word in the language that could be used in any advertising medium and people would automatically read, listen, or watch what was to follow. Of course, you cannot do that. Not because it would be construed necessarily as vulgar, but because it would be boring if we all did it. Yet, the word has power. And it is such power you look for in all advertising, as well as in the medium you choose to transmit your message. The power to gain attention. The power to attract interest. The power to persuade.

When boy and girl meet, and they are attracted to each other, what happens? They try to gain each other's attention in the most demonstrable way possible. They flirt with their eyes. The message is clear and sends a strong signal because the eyes are a powerful medium. Once they have gained that attention, then they talk. And the conversation on both sides is geared to attract and win interest. It is nearly always positive. It is meant to influence. It is often seductive. If the conversation achieves its end, then the medium of speech is working effectively for both. However, if one or the other trips or falls, boasts or babbles, all may be lost. Either may use body language, which communicates interest in a visual, tactile way.

Then comes the ultimate test. One person or the other has to cross the barrier to assure interest has been truly gained. It can be done in many ways: "Are you going to be here tomorrow?" "Can I treat you to something?" "May I phone you?" "Can I see you home?" "Would you like to go out with me?" Which question is asked depends on how far one believes one can go. And the timing must be right. The visual setting must be conducive. The mood appropriate.

The same in advertising. The message and the medium must work together to achieve a single purpose. All the factors involved in any girl-boy mating situation present the same challenges and opportunities as in advertising products or services. In both, what you say, how you say it, where you say it, with what sincerity you say it, all are collectively vital to success.

So there, I've said it again.

CHAPTER
SEVEN

Max, Don't Make Trouble

As with all people who migrate to new countries, eventually part of the immigrant's culture is absorbed into the mainstream. We are the better off for it because it allows our language and our customs to grow and become richer for the experience. It is as true of Jews as it is of Italians, Chinese, Irish, or Jamaicans. We all begin to borrow from each other. Sometimes it is food, other times it is humour or music. Often it is language itself. For instance, such words as "schnozzle", "schmuck", "schnook", "schmoose", and "shtick", now used by many people, are derived from Yiddish. The black people originated many of our musical terms like jazz, ragtime, boogie woogie, and the non-musical nitty gritty.

Being brought up in a good Jewish family, I was steeped in culture. I could read and understand Yiddish. I could speak and sing it. I think that helped when I entered advertising because some of the cadence and expressions of the language spilled over into many of the advertising campaigns we did on behalf of clients. It wasn't that we borrowed directly from Yiddish, it was more that it influenced our style of expressing ourselves in English.

It was also significant that, after the Second World War, a large number of Jews found their way into advertising in New York. They, themselves, brought a sense of Jewish language and humour to the business. Words like "shtick" and "shmata" became commonplace. By the time I arrived on the scene, it was part and parcel of advertising creativity. After all, New York then was the hub of the advertising world. Largely we were not breaking new ground in Canada, but following their tradition.

The title for my first book came from a line delivered

by a Jewish tailor in a TV commercial "Have I ever lied to you before?" Given the proper inflection, it said a lot to most viewers. It made the question real because people could identify with it, no matter who they were. Granted it was Jewish, but it was also recognizable and, therefore, credible. If it wasn't said with a Yiddish inflection though, it would have meant a lot less.

The same could be said for one of our more famous slogans, but far more subtly. That was for Speedy Muffler King. When we developed "At Speedy, You're a Somebody," I took it to the client, who was himself Jewish. He liked it, but he was concerned. "Jerry," he said, "it's bad grammar. It should be, 'You're a somebody at Speedy.' Besides that, it's too Jewish." What he meant was that the inflection within the phrase was a common way of expressing oneself in Yiddish. It took me about two months to convince him this was the slogan he needed for his business.

I've used Jewish humour as a shield and guardian angel all my life. For example, when I was 17 years old and in high school I weighed 115 pounds. In order to buy books and clothes and help Mother feed me during the following semester, I started hunting for a job. I came across the following advertisement in *The Toronto Telegram*:

> Lumberjacks wanted. Must be experienced, very strong, able to tolerate long working hours in the bush. Good pay. Apply in person at Marathon Paper in Marathon, Ontario situated on Lake Superior.

I hitchhiked up to Marathon. It took me 2½ days. I got there bitten by black flies, hungry, tired, but filled with determination to get the job.

I located the foreman and presented myself as a job applicant. He took one look at me and burst into uncontrollable laughter:

"You skinny runt. How dare you take up my time? You couldn't cut down a twig let alone a tree. So get lost."

I responded with controlled indignation. "Give me an axe and give me a chance. I've hitchhiked all the way from Toronto for this job." The foreman pointed at an axe planted in an oak tree. The tree was at least 4 feet in diameter. I yanked the axe out of the tree, mustered all my strength, took five swipes at the tree and down it came.

In stunned disbelief, the foreman looked down his nose

at me and blared out, "a freak of nature. Obviously the tree had dry rot."

"OK," I replied, "point me at a healthier one and a bigger one."

"There," spat out the foreman. "Get that one." It was another oak but about 7 feet in diameter and much, much taller. Once again I dug deep into my diminished reservoir of strength and in eight swipes at the tree, down it came crashing just feet from the foreman.

"Holy God, you skinny runt. Where the hell did you learn to cut down trees like that? I've never seen anything like it."

"In the Sahara Forest," I coyly answered.

"The Saharan Forest? Don't you mean the Sahara Desert?" I looked the foreman in the eye, flipped the axe into the ground and responded:

"Sure, *now* it's a desert."

I bring this up for only one reason. It's not to get all copywriters to begin studying Yiddish idioms. In Canada, we need a greater diversification within advertising so we can begin to express ourselves in the most delightful human ways possible. And it is just not the words, but different attitudes and perspectives, greater breadth to the visual images, and more diversity in the music. What kind of advertising would we get if every copywriter and art director in the business was over sixty years of age? More to the point, what would we be missing? We would be missing youth, the way the young express themselves. The visual images, the sound tracks would be from Lord only knows what era. And our advertising, our marketing would suffer.

Why aren't we enticing more and more women into the business, especially in art directing and copywriting? Whether they are young or old, or in between, they have a different perspective than the male of the species. It should be nurtured; it should be encouraged. I do not give a damn if most of the clients are still males. You are not supposed to write and produce ads for clients, but for consumers.

Women have an equal role to play in the advertising business because they can bring a fresh, different approach to it. They look at the world from a different point of view. They are probably far more sympathetic to consumers, which doesn't mean they are pussycats, but more sensitive to consumer likes and dislikes. And they are as intelligent as males

— with enough emotional sensitivity that makes them ideal for planning and creating exciting, new, breakthrough advertising.

You want an example of Yiddish humour combined with an untapped awesome power of female guile? Read on.

Irving and Bessie had just retired for the night and Irving was in the mood for a little affection. If you know what I mean. As it happens, Bessie wasn't.

Irving: "Bessie darling, lift up the nightgown."

Nothing. No response.

Irving again: "Bessie sweetheart, please lift up the nightgown."

Icy silence.

Irving with an edge in his voice: "Bessie, you're getting me angry. If you don't lift up the nightgown, I'm leaving this bedroom."

No response. Nothing.

Irving leaped out of bed in a rage, opened the door, slamming it shut behind him. Bessie tiptoed out of bed and locked the door. Fifteen minutes passed. Bessie heard a gentle tapping on the door, accompanied by a muted, "Bessie darling. Please open the door. It's me, your loving husband, Irving."

Again stony silence.

Louder tapping and with anger in his voice, Irving cried out, "Bessie, it's your sweetheart. Please unlock the door."

Bessie, still ignoring the request, turned over and shut her eyes again.

This time loud fist-pounding landed on the door. Irving screamed out, "Bessie, if you don't unlock the door, I swear to you I'm going to smash it down."

At long last Bessie spoke.

"Listen to him. . . . Can't lift up a nightgown and he's going to smash down a door."

Although more women have entered the business in recent years, there are still not enough of them. Furthermore, they haven't been given the responsibilities they deserve. They haven't been allowed to grow at a pace the industry requires. At a time when creativity needs a real boost, I believe women could be the pioneers in a new period of excellence in advertising. Only in this century did they get the vote. Late in this century they should be given the greatest opportunity possible to move marketing and advertising into a new era.

What can be said for women in advertising, can also be said for our newer immigrants, too. If the Yiddish language and its humour has contributed a bit to the role of advertising in our society, then other races, other language groups have their contributions to make as well.

In the Jewish community in which I grew up, it was the male who ventured forth into the business world to make his mark, not the woman. That has changed dramatically. I know. I have three fabulous children and they're all off running the way they want to go. I have a daughter, Leslie, who is a pediatrician, a son David, who is a lawyer, and son, Noah, who has just graduated from the University of Western Ontario.

In most ethnic communities now, both males and females are given a better chance to reach whatever heights are possible for them. I applaud that. The advertising industry should applaud it too, and take advantage of it.

Let me end with a Yiddish story, even though it dates back to a time during World War II when Jews were fighting for their survival.

Two Jewish partisans are about to be executed by a Nazi firing squad. Just before the German officer gives the order to fire, one prisoner shrieks: "Wait, wait. I demand my rights. I insist on a blindfold." The other prisoner turns to him and whispers urgently, "For God's sake, Max, don't make trouble."

This is a time for making trouble. I believe the business I dearly love is imperilled unless it moves with the times.

I'll meet you at the barricades.

CHAPTER
EIGHT

Is This the Party to Whom
I Am Speaking?

• Accompanying your monthly credit card billing (almost any card) you find one or a number of small, colourful brochures advertising unrelated products you may purchase through it.

• In the mail one day you get a glossy catalogue from Mountain Equipment Co-op (25,000 mail orders in 1989) or any of a growing number of similar firms, with a comprehensive listing of products you can order through the mail.

• You're watching a local television station and an ad comes on the screen saying you can buy a certain book, a cassette of a well-known rock artist's music, or a videotape on how to improve your golf just by dialling a 1-800 number and paying by money order or credit card.

• A four-page brochure is stuck in your door that advertises Chinese food at a new takeout restaurant in your neighbourhood; or a one-page flyer arrives from a local contractor who installs aluminum siding.

• You receive a phone call from a person who asks if you would be interested in having spring water — or some other product — in your home as a substitute for drinking tap water; both the dispenser unit and the water bottles to be delivered directly to your home.

• You check out at the local supermarket and receive a computer-printed coupon for a discount on a specific product, or you receive a booklet by mail with numerous money-back coupons in it.

What do all these advertising vehicles have in common? They are part of the fast-growing industry called Direct Marketing, estimated presently in Canada to be worth seven billion dollars per year. And growing. You may like it, you may dislike it; one thing for sure, you are going to see more of it in the coming years because it is one of the most powerful marketing techniques now available to Canadian manufacturers, retailers, and service organizations. Even governments.

It is not a new medium. It has been popular among large retail chains since the turn of the century. As I wrote in the history of Canadian advertising for Mel Hurtig's *Canadian Encyclopedia*: The most effective vehicle (in 1900) for fostering a national market was the mail-order catalogue, especially Eaton's. Not an advertising medium in the strict sense of the word (because space was not for sale), the seasonal catalogues reached millions of farm and town people with advertising for a wide range of merchandise.

Direct marketing not only reaches farm and town people but those in the major metropolitan areas as well. And it does it in an imaginative number of inexpensive ways. Indeed, it is one of the fastest-growing service industries in North America. As Jeffrey Hallet, president of Trend Response and Analysis Company, a leading U.S. research company, summed it up a couple of years ago: "An entirely new set of dynamics is emerging that will dictate success and failure in the marketplace of the late '80s and beyond. The protocols, techniques, methods, and assumptions that have formed the foundation of sound marketing may no longer be relied upon." From my own research (and that of others), I know the promotional and direct marketing budgets of many Canadian corporations now represent as much as sixty per cent of their media advertising. Such promotional spending is projected to overtake that of media expenditures by the year 2000.

The reason it is growing at such a rapid rate is that mass media campaigns are just not good enough to meet the ever-changing needs of many corporate clients. Nor is a simple combination of attention-grabbing creativity and appropriate media selection all that is required to attain and sustain success for many product categories. The era of mass advertising, based on the premise that big is better and more is best, is being questioned, even among products and services traditionally marketed that way.

Over the past decade or so, we have witnessed a revolution in both the technologies of marketing and the transmissions of pertinent sales messages to specialized groups of qualified prospects. We now have better means of defining and delineating such audiences efficiently as well as more effective ways of reaching them inexpensively. If you have a list of people who own recreational vehicles, they have something in common. Therefore, you can directly market products compatible with their interests. They represent a market, one that is less expensive to reach by mail than through broadly based media advertising. As well, you can measure both the cost and the effectiveness of the program because there is a direct relationship between the number of people on your list, the expenditure required to reach them, and the sales you eventually generate. In fact, we are now capable of breaking down our population more precisely into specific market segments, whether it be male or female, young or old, homeowners or not.

With the advent of the Canadian postal code, the segmentation possibilities became even greater. The first three digits of the postal code designate the initial distribution points for mail sorting in the post office. These are called forward sortation areas, and there are 1,250 of them across the country with between 4,500 and 5,000 households in each. Coincident with this technological revolution, which was mainly inspired by the growth of computer capacities and capabilities, we also have more and more products being developed that are of interest to clearly defined demographic groups.

This new approach to product development has been accelerated by burgeoning changes in perceived lifestyles. A greater emphasis, for example, on sport, exercise, and fitness has produced demand for all kinds of new or upgraded products associated with an active life. New attitudes on health and nutrition have altered eating habits, and changed consumer buying preferences. A more casual outlook on lifestyle has revolutionized our approach to fashion, home entertainment, and hobbies. The accelerated pace of living has meant most of us have less time to go browsing in stores for products or services we might be interested in if we happen to run across them. And the diversity of products now available has increased dramatically.

Indeed, the various media themselves have had an enormous influence on how we perceive ourselves within society. Articles and programs appear almost daily, pointing out new trends, redefining individual expectations, resolving perceived group problems. The Yuppie lifestyle. Retired people. Working mothers. Then there is public opinion research, which regularly tracks, among other things, the evolving patterns of living styles. And many new products and services reflect those changing perceptions and patterns accurately.

At the same time, we have individually become more selective and sophisticated in our purchase patterns. No longer can the producers of goods and services look on the public as an amorphous mass of undiscriminating sheep, forced to accept whatever is available. Large segments of the public now view themselves as individual purchasers with individual needs and desires. What better way to fulfill those needs and desires than by talking to them on a one-to-one basis?

Mass marketing makes less and less sense in such a fractured environment. The expenditure of inordinate amounts of money only to create an awareness of products and services is too expensive, too difficult to measure in efficiency, and too inflexible to meet the demands of many producers of goods. What companies want is to reach market clusters, or micro-markets, of similar potential buyers.

Direct marketing is strategic marketing. It means looking at a product or service from the point of view of who is more prone to want it and buy it, and what is the best way to reach that potential purchaser. Strategic marketing ignores any advertising agency bias in planning a specific strategy. There is a pronounced bias within most ad agencies since their profits are based mainly on the commissions generated by media advertising. The trend is to a more diverse, more selective program that incorporates a more balanced approach, a more provocative thrust to product marketing.

One distinct advantage of direct marketing is that you can tailor your sales message more directly, explain the features of the products in greater detail, and show the applications of their use more graphically. You can't do that for most products in a 30- or 60-second commercial, but you can do it in a well-written brochure or flyer. Indeed, in direct marketing, you *have* to be more explicit in explaining your product. Potential customers do not have the advantage of picking it up, looking it over, and deciding whether they like what they see, be it the quality, the price, or even the colour. And there is no salesperson from whom to elicit specific information. All the pertinent questions must be answered in the direct-marketing copy.

One product, for example, has been offered to a wide audience through direct marketing. It is simple, inexpensive, yet an item a manufacturer might have great difficulty promoting through mass marketing because expenditures could be totally out of proportion to both production costs and profit. It's an adjustable photocell sensor that turns lights on in your home as it gets dark, turns them off as it gets lighter. With greater concern over home security, it is a product that should be attractive to many homeowners. To operate it, all you have to do is plug a lamp into it, then plug it into any standard outlet. It features, as the direct-mail piece says, "100% solid-state circuitry with a built-in electronic photocell sensor which constantly monitors changes in light."

Now, this particular product, offered by Shell Canada to its credit card holders in 1989, is so inexpensive that selling it one at a time just wouldn't be practical. Therefore, potential customers were offered a set of three at a price of $39.95 per set in a single payment (or $12.04 in four equal monthly installments), plus handling and shipping charges of $5.95. Provincial sales taxes were extra, depending on the purchaser's province. Payment was simple because the customer already had a credit card. The envelope-size, four-page, four-colour pamphlet offering the product was piggybacked with the Shell monthly billing to credit card holders, which meant the cost of marketing was minimal. As well, the pamphlet stated: "Please allow up to four weeks for delivery." Therefore, the distributor has no need to warehouse a large inventory, and production could easily be geared to response, reducing costs again.

To market such an item initially through hardware stores across the country would cost a great deal more than doing it by direct mail, and the manufacturer would have to support such a product introduction through advertising, either alone or in conjunction with a number of leading hardware chains. Having done this, the customer would still have to go out and find the product before a purchase was made.

On the other hand, if the direct marketing campaign is successful, the manufacturer already has one foot in the door with customers, another foot in the door with future retailers.

You can say that this example is over-simplified. Yet it illustrates graphically why direct marketing can be so advantageous as compared to traditional mass-media advertising and initial distribution through retail outlets. And the number of products and services being marketed in this way is practically limitless: from food and clothing to entertainment equipment and handyman tools; from books and records to insurance and travel.

Most direct marketing in Canada — and we are still far behind the U.S. in its application — is done in one of three ways. First, like Shell, there are companies that issue credit cards for one reason or another. When direct marketing products, they act as middlepersons, piggybacking products of others onto their own required mailings for the mutual profit of both. Then there are the distributors of products and services who act as the direct sales organization, either through catalogues that are sent to a specific list of predetermined, potential buyers, or through a combination of catalogues and store outlets. Finally, there are the producers of goods who, working in conjunction with direct-marketing specialists, merchandise their goods in any one of numerous ways: e.g., local mail or media advertising to reach a predetermined audience in a specific locale, direct mail to certain selected demographic groups, or telemarketing over the phone to similar groups.

The key to success in all such enterprises is to reach the greatest potential audience of probable buyers with a product that will interest them, at a price that will intrigue them, and to do it in the most alluring way possible.

A well-defined audience is a prerequisite in all direct marketing. In fact, it has become a science over the past two decades. What it requires is segmentation, the process of differentiating among groups or segments of people. Depending on the product or service being sold, the segmentation can be broad or narrow. For small local retailers, it could be designated postal walks of residences within their immediate area; for larger ones, the whole city, a region, or the province. For manufacturers, the best route may be through piggybacking on credit card billings. But distinctions must be made. An oil company card has a broader base than, say, those who hold an American Express Gold Card. Both demand some form of credit rating, but, because the Gold

Card offer much wider spending powers, the rating will be more restrictive. And the products offered through each will, in most cases, be equally restricted. Then there are designated lists: e.g., professionals, such as doctors and dentists; interest groups, such as hobbyists or sports participants; magazine subscription groups. The possibilities are endless. The science comes in matching the right group to the right product.

One of the major problems with direct marketing for the consumer is that you and I may be on lists we don't give a damn about. We may be solicited endlessly to buy products or services we have absolutely no interest in. That is what we call "junk mail". For most direct marketers, junk mail is a cross they don't want to bear because it tarnishes the image of the profession. That is why accurate market segmentation is so important. The better the demographics of the list, the less the antagonism generated among recipients. Needless to say, the less waste too. Still the problem occurs because lists are often sold by the originator to other direct marketers, often merged with still further lists until the vital demographic profile of customers begins to dissipate.

Here is a personal account of an associate of mine who understands both the efficacy of direct marketing and its weaknesses. A number of years ago he decided to make subtle adjustments to his name on his credit cards. If his full name was William Stephen Smith, he would apply for various cards under William Smith, William S. Smith, Bill Smith, W.S. Smith, et cetera. All quite legal, but it gave him the advantage of being able to tell — with reasonable certainty — whether his name on a certain credit card had been sold to another company or direct mail distributor. Sure enough, soon after being accepted as a credit card holder with one specific company, he began receiving mail under that particular name designation from companies he had never dealt with. It was obvious his name, along with the entire list, was being sold. Most of what he received he considered to be junk mail. What he did then was write the original company asking them to delete his name from subsequent sales of their lists. He received a polite reply saying that his wishes would be adhered to — and the unsolicited mailings soon stopped.

Most of us don't have the acumen to take such steps to protect ourselves from junk mail. The more our names appear on lists, the more potential we have of ending up on other lists, ones we may have no desire to be on at all. Some lists are highly protected because they represent a select audience. Others are brokered around. That is a shame because it devalues the relationship between the company or organization and the original customer. If, however, you do not know who to blame, does it make a difference?

It sure as hell does. It demeans direct marketing. It makes people suspicious of such sales techniques. After all, consumers don't give a sweet kidney about how you reach him or her. All they care about is what you are saying to them, and whether it is pertinent or irrelevant. Many consumers are becoming awash in junk mail. And their immediate reaction is to throw it out in the recyclable garbage. That is because too many direct marketing practitioners are employing techniques that are inappropriate and indiscriminate.

Another example. An acquaintance decided to donate money to a certain charitable organization for the first time. Within weeks she was inundated with requests for donations from other such organizations. I have no problem with charities soliciting funds; but I have serious reservations about them trading names back and forth as if it were some kind of game. (I hope that isn't so.) If my acquaintance's experience is any indication, it means it is happening. I would suggest strongly that such organizations desist from the practice because it's turning people off.

Admittedly, there is a vicarious thrill to shopping through direct mail. Most of us would describe this process in the following way: "I saw it, it intrigued me. I read about it, it convinced me. I bought it, and I found I liked it." When this happens, the feeling is one akin to receiving a birthday present. The simple opening of the package can bring pleasure.

That is the feeling that should accompany all direct marketing, whether it be an alarm-clock radio, a cassette recording, or a box of lobsters. When that feeling is one of pleasure, then the customer is more apt to purchase other products and services through the same system. In effect, they become devoted armchair shoppers. In order for that prospective customer to cross that threshold, however, the material he or she receives must be interesting and informative, concise yet detailed, and graphically presented. Although there are continuing problems with who receives which offer, the most significant obstacle to successful direct marketing lies within the presentation of the product or service itself. Quality lists are important, quality creativity in the presentation is imperative.

In direct marketing, art and copywriting are dissimilar from advertising. Creative people must learn to follow a more disciplined marketing plan in a direct market situation because the audience is more restricted. They must be able to visualize the benefits of the product or service in a more provocative way because they get only one chance at showing it. They must be able to explain its benefits more precisely and concisely because there is no one available to answer additional questions.

Unfortunately, many of the creative people working on direct marketing campaigns are young and inexperienced because it is considered an unromantic occupation. It doesn't have the glamour and prestige of big-budget advertising. Indeed, for many, writing catalogue copy is the first job one gets in the business. It is dull and boring — almost as boring as writing want ads. Anyone with a sense of their own worth wants to get as far away as possible from what they perceive to be a laborious and uncreative form of advertising.

However, as more and more dollars are being poured into it, creative people are beginning to rethink their roles. Slowly, but surely, design and copy are beginning to reflect the ascendancy of the new marketing kid on the block — and new creative teams are finding it a unique, not irksome challenge.

Telemarketing is included in direct marketing. Quite simply, it is using the telephone for selling or servicing people and businesses. No one has any trouble with the servicing angle, especially people outside the major metropolitan areas. Most people who live in a major Canadian city have no idea what Bell's 800 Service Directory is. That's because they can simply pick up their local phone book and find the company they want to call. If, however, you live in a smaller centre only a short distance away, then you probably not only have a copy of the directory, but you use it frequently. It is the way to make direct contact with firms whose offices are elsewhere.

The Bell service directory I have has more than one hundred white pages and double that number in yellow pages. For instance, if you wish to contact (the late) Eastern Airlines, you can find the 1-800 number of their Canadian head office in Montreal. If you are in Ontario and you want to talk to Purolator Courier in Red Deer, you can find the number there, too. If you have a craving to go on a windjammer cruise, you may dial the direct number of Barefoot Cruises in Miami.

Although many of the listings have to do with business-to-business communications, just as many — if not more — deal with public enquiries. Some have restrictions on their call areas, whether provinces or specific area codes. That is because their client base is limited to where the majority resides. Some are strictly for soliciting business, others are hot-lines for existing customers.

One of the problems Canadians face is the fact they cannot access many U.S. 800 numbers, even though the promotional material received in Canada lists the number. An amusing one is the 800 number of the American Telemarketing Association in California. It is not accessible from Canada. At the same time, many American firms now have cross-border numbers, or a separate in-Canada one.

Certainly, telemarketing is a fast-rising business, estimated at about one billion dollars per year in Canada. And that is undoubtedly a gross understatement since it only encompasses the solicitation of individuals by phone. Lord only knows how much order processing (hotels, theatre tickets, magazine subscriptions) is done over 1-800 lines advertising through normal media channels. Nor does it take into consideration corporate sales support; using business long distance or WATS (WATS stand for "Wide Area Telephone Service". A business buys a block of time [5, 10, 15 hours] from Bell Canada and makes the time available free of charge to anyone who wants to be in touch with that business. Time in excess of that purchased is billed to the business at a predetermined cost per hour) to reach certain customers on orders or re-orders rather than visiting them.

Telemarketing is here to stay, despite its obvious flaws, which are far more encumbering than those in directing marketing by mail. There is no industry standard about when telemarketers may make a call to a residence to sell something, although there are suggested guidelines. That means you and I could get a call at eleven o'clock at night, or eight o'clock in the morning on a weekend. That is intrusive. And unlike other direct marketers, who have a system for you to be excluded from direct mail, you can't phone a hot-line and request you receive no more telephone solicitations. Not yet anyway. Finally, the CRTC has imposed restrictions specifically on the automatic-dialling machines used in much direct marketing. The problem is that the regulations are almost impossible to enforce.

Yet, despite these faults, the business is bound to grow. One company sells products and services by phone to only upper-income families, a group you would think was the toughest to sell in this way. Yet it works. Why? Simply because the company selects only those items that have a high quality, are not easily obtainable through regular market channels, and because it is prompt with its deliveries. There is also a domino effect to such upscale selling. Once one family has made a purchase — and is satisfied with the product — then it is far easier to make a second, and a third sale. In addition, that family will tell the neighbours of the service and you get other people who want to be on the bandwagon. One of the best examples is food. Steaks, lobsters, cheeses, wines; indeed a wide range of such items can be sold — and are being sold — over the phone. But, again, the quality and service must automatically be built in if you are to be successful. You can even sell fresh eggs by phone.

Telemarketing is only an extension of the phone power many have used for years. The key to success in the real estate business is to get listings. How do you do that? Simple. You cold-call people and ask them if they are interested in selling their house or buying another one. Or, if a homeowner is trying to sell his or her house privately, you pitch them on the benefits of having a realtor work for them. In real estate it's been going on for years because it is the most proficient way to get leads. The same can be said for newspaper and magazine subscriptions. Or life insurance. It even works in the advertising business. I've gained many accounts by simply picking up the phone and pitching a potential client.

Now almost everybody is in the game, either directly or through a telemarketing company. Any business from a bank to a cosmetic firm. From a conglomerate of restaurants to a water-softening firm. Why? Because it is economical. With an efficient computerized database and a number of trained telephone operators, telemarketing is a most cost-efficient means of selling a large array of products and services. And, as in other forms of direct marketing, you can easily measure your costs against your sales to see if it is working well.

As the technology of telecommunications becomes more sophisticated, so does its uses for telemarketers. In automated call-processing, you dial a particular number and get a computerized message. The message may be information on a product or service, or it may be designed to trigger a potential response. The computer can do it all, whether it is geared to sending you further information by mail, or taking your order. All you need is a touchtone phone to tap into it. Certain surveys in the U.S. have found that people would far prefer to deal with a computer than a live person. Why? Because they rarely get a busy signal, are never put on hold, and the service is available twenty-four hours a day.

All of us have become far more linked to direct marketing than we care to admit. You want tickets to a new musical that's coming to town? You don't necessarily go to the theatre as you used to. You pick up the phone and order them, giving your credit card name and number as payment. You wish to reserve golf or tennis time? You don't drive to the club, you pick up the phone and do it. You clip coupons out of a newspaper or magazine for a special cents-off deal on a product advertised by either one of your local supermarkets or the producers themselves. You have a complaint about a product. What do you do? You simply pick up the phone and dial the company's number. If you live some distance from it, there is probably a 1-800 number to get in touch with them directly. Or, even if you are happy with the product and want to re-order a part or an addition, you use the same number and the product is delivered to you by courier — often free of charge. You go into a store and someone offers you a free sample. You try it, you like it, you buy it. That's direct marketing, too.

Direct marketing surrounds us. We are exposed to it almost every day. Is it any wonder, then, that it is being employed more and more to sell products and services? Of course not. What do you expect — privacy? Well, only if you stop your mail, cut off your phone, never respond to an advertisement, give up your credit cards, and buy everything with cash. And, even if you do all that, you'll still probably end up on a list somewhere.

Sorry folks. I think it is called "free enterprise."

CHAPTER NINE

To Hell With Getting Better, Let's Get Bigger

During 1989 in Canada, the following advertising agency mergers or acquisitions occurred:

• McKim Advertising, of Toronto, Canada's oldest advertising agency, sold a forty per cent share of its company to N.W. Ayer, New York.

• Schur Peppler, Toronto, joined W.B. Doner, Detroit, to become Doner Schur Peppler.

• U.S.-dominated Marketel/McCann-Erickson, Montreal, merged with Publicité Foster to emerge as Marketel/Foster/McCann-Erickson (imagine being the switchboard operator there).

• Carder Gray Advertising, of Toronto, was purchased by DDB Needham Worldwide, Troy, Michigan. Ranked number eleven in the world, DDB is the operating arm of Omnicom, which, in turn is reportedly the third largest agency in the world with billings of some $2.5 billion. And, in case you didn't know, the DDB used to stand for Doyle Dane Bernbach, one of the most imaginative, creative agencies in the world. Since it merged with Needham in 1988, it has been reduced to three unimaginative initials. Criminal.

• Palmer Bonner, Toronto, in business no more than ten years, sold a majority interest to Bozell, New York.

• Miller Myers Bruce DallaCosta, Toronto, sold a minority interest to Lopex, London, U.K., an international operation with reported billings in the neighbourhood of $800 million, and part of the umbrella group, Alliance International. Confusing isn't it?

And. . .

• Goodis & Sharabura merged with Lowe Case Associates, of Toronto, an independent unit of the Spectrum Group, which — believe it or not — is a holding company of the aforementioned McKim Advertising. Are you still with me?

In the international field, the WPP Group of England, now the largest agency worldwide, bought the U.S. giant, The Ogilvy Group. In Canada that affected two agencies: Ogilvy and Mather, and Scali McCabe Sloves Inc. Back in 1987, WPP made world headlines when it purchased the 100-year-old U.S. firm, J. Walter Thompson.

If you are not in the business, most of these names will mean little or nothing to you. On the other hand, it gives you an indication of what has been happening to the advertising business at an increasingly accelerated pace. It's called merger mania, and it has been occurring now for more than two decades. At the level it has reached now, it doesn't bode well for the business or the profession. On the business side, it means more and more accounts in fewer and fewer hands, with global campaigns being churned out irrespective of where they will be read, heard, or seen. It won't be Big Brother Is Watching You, but Big Brother Is Selling You. For the profession, it means less and less individuality, greater bureaucracy, even possibly censorship of ideas.

One sad story makes a point about merger mania.

A friend, Bruno Rubess, was, at the time I'm talking about, president of Volkswagen Canada. He is now a senior corporate officer with the company at its head office in Wolfsburg, Germany. I was in Bruno's office one particular day in 1986 discussing a marketing proposal; I wasn't getting his full attention. He seemed distracted. That just wasn't like him. When I asked if there was something wrong with my report, he replied that there wasn't, sat back for a moment, and then suddenly unleashed a savage outburst of bitterness, anger, and sarcasm. The object of his attack was his advertising agency, Doyle Dane Bernbach.

He had received a call from the agency that morning informing him that it was merging with Needham Harper and Steers. The news came as no surprise since the announcement of the forthcoming marriage had been in the advertising trade papers for weeks. What, then, had set him off? The agency had just explained that there was a conflict of interest which had to be resolved. Needham had the Honda account while Doyle Dane represented Volkswagen. The new company hadn't made up its mind which one to keep. That was the point of the conversation. Even I was shocked at the effrontery of the agency people to make such a call.

Bruno was apoplectic. How dare they, he wanted to know, tell him whether his company was good enough to be their account? How dare they treat a client that way? I had never seen Bruno that angry, and frustrated. A couple of days later, he heard from the agency again. He was informed it had decided to keep the Volkswagen business. Bruno thanked him profusely for their kindness, thoughtfulness, and loyalty. I can imagine the sarcasm with which he said it. Even when he told me of the conversation later, I winced. And I don't do that easily. The story speaks volumes about the arrogance, insensitivity, and business ethnics of modern mega-agencies. They feel they rule the world, and clients will tremble whenever they ordain to make a decision.

The fact is that no one in the worldwide Volkswagen organization has the authority to fire their advertising agency except the Chairman at the Wolfsburg, Germany, headquarters. Had Bruno had the authority, they would have been history!

The incongruity that struck me at the time of the Rubess incident was the fact that both agencies had grown to a point where each was becoming a cumbersome monolith. All of a sudden they were merging to create an even bigger monster. I didn't know that much about Needham then; but Doyle Dane Bernbach was as familiar to me as my own agency. As I've told you, Bill Bernbach was my American mentor. The agency had done wonderful things for Volkswagen. It had successfully promoted that admittedly ugly little beetlelike car into a household name in the U.S. Now it had expanded to such a point that top management could no longer control much of what was going on by virtue of its size. Yet it was merging with another huge agency to become even more unwieldy.

Remember that as part of my education in the advertising culture I sat at the knee of William Bernbach, whose agency crafted the original Volkswagen advertising. He is the one who taught me that you cannot write a proper advertisement unless you know the product intimately, know how it is made, believe in its efficacy, and tell the truth about it. To meet these ends Bill always sent a writer and an art director directly into the plant where his agency's products were manufactured.

Think small.

Our little car isn't so much of a novelty any more.

A couple of dozen college kids don't try to squeeze inside it.

The guy at the gas station doesn't ask where the gas goes.

Nobody even stares at our shape.

In fact, some people who drive our little flivver don't even think 32 miles to the gallon is going any great guns.

Or using five pints of oil instead of five quarts.

Or never needing anti-freeze.

Or racking up 40,000 miles on a set of tires.

That's because once you get used to some of our economies, you don't even think about them any more.

Except when you squeeze into a small parking spot. Or renew your small insurance. Or pay a small repair bill. Or trade in your old VW for a new one.

Think it over.

Volkswagen magazine advertisement. Agency Doyle Dane Bernbach, New York

As an example, Julian Koenig and George Lois visited Wolfsburg, Germany, and literally lived in the plant watching Volkswagens being put together. One day a foreman ordered a Volkswagen off the line and sent it back to the paint shop. Julian (with whom I later on struck up a friendship) asked the foreman what was wrong with the car. He could see no flaws. The foreman pointed out a small scratch on the glove compartment. That is how the famous Volkswagen ad whose headline read "Lemon" was born.

Taking advantage of the ugliness of the car, Doyle Dane Bernbach and its creative people were up-front in their advertising about the odd appearance of the car. They concentrated on VW's superb gas mileage, low maintenance, no need to fill the radiator with water, and, of course, its ungainly appearance. That is how the ad entitled "Think Small" was born. In television one of the most dramatic and effective VW spots showed a Volkswagen driving up a mountain through a heavy snowstorm for the entire first 55 seconds of the spot. The Volkswagen parked in front of a snowplough and the announcer simply uttered the words, "Did you ever wonder how the man who drives the snowplough gets to the snowplough?" Wonderful. Compelling. Clear. Memorable. Classic.

Size, up to a point, has advantages. After all, in 1975, I merged Goodis Goldberg Soren with the grande dame of Canadian advertising, MacLaren. But the terms had been different. At least, at the time, I thought they were different. The point is that an ad agency is built on two key ingredients: its relationship with its clients and its creative output on behalf of those clients. When an agency becomes too large, handling too many accounts, perhaps operating in a number of countries, then a bureaucratic vision of client relations begins to take over. Agency costs are cut by flogging the same creativity everywhere it is doing business: Canada, the United States, England, France — wherever. The almighty commission on media expenditures takes precedence over doing what is best for the client. Skewed research — done at a profit, of course — proves you are on the right track, whatever that track may be. Memos fly back and forth in a convoluted flurry of neatly diagrammed nonsense. In other words, bullshit baffles brains.

If you are a major corporation you end up having agency

number-crunchers speaking to company number-crunchers. You no longer know who is responsible for what. If you have a dominant brand, it will still continue to dominate even though significant erosion may take place. That means your market, like the weather, is variable with some overcast, but you hope, improving. And no one trusts the weatherman.

If you are an up-and-coming company — and you understand marketing — you will recognize the short shrift you are getting from the megalith and move to a smaller, more responsive agency. And, if such a breakup occurs, the announcement in the trade papers will state: "We couldn't see eye-to-eye on a fundamental matter involving the creative approach." In other words, we have had enough of mumbo-jumbo incompetence, irresolution, and inordinate billings.

Economies of scale may work in other industries, but, in advertising, they begin to defeat the agency's purpose by placing revenues before client needs, by assuming that every potential consumer is the same, whether they be English-speaking or French-speaking, whether they live on the east coast or the west coast, whether they be American or Canadian. It matters not to the number-crunchers in agency management as long as the ads are flashily expensive and media costs generate maximum commissions. It is the age-old story of greed, and it is happening in my business through national, international, and worldwide mergers. It is like a plague that gets transported from one country to another. The sad part is that nobody (except Bruno Rubess) seems to give a damn. And just as many clients are in the dark because, more often than not, they simply consider the ad agency, at best, a necessary evil.

In the beginning, many such mergers made sense. When a manufacturing company was expanding into the international market, it was logical to retain the same agency as it opened up new territories rather than explaining its objectives to new people time and time again. The agencies reacted favorably to these opportunities, initially by opening their own offices in each new country. Soon, however, the advantages of the acquisition route became apparent. More often than not it was less expensive to acquire a small local agency and, along with it, talent indigenous to the country, as well as additional new accounts.

This was a new game. As the trend grew, many agencies hired financial people who could better plot mergers and takeovers. It not only helped the bottom line, but it made such agencies feel they were Goliaths of the business, with their nameplates on many buildings in many countries and their letterheads boasting of their growing network of offices. It even helped to attract other multinational clients.

What the principals in these companies and the money managers who worked for them failed to understand, or at least take into account, was the fact that any advertising agency is the sum of its work done on behalf of other companies. It is a service business whose success is based solely on the talent of its people. It does not have great wealth in real estate, or huge landholdings to develop at a later date. Neither does it have much capital equipment nor production lines based on wholly owned patents. In advertising, the way you treat your people is imperative to your success. As well, most ad agencies were not public companies with thousands of shareholders, but privately owned. Therefore, assets were, to a certain extent, limited. The temptation of a merger could look great as far as instant wealth was concerned.

Once the acquisition route was opened, it became obvious to crafty individuals that advertising agencies — regardless of size — were comparatively easy prey to takeovers. You just had to be able to pull the right financial levers. Partners in agencies could be lured into mergers with the promise of immediate capital gains, stock options, and the other paraphernalia of the takeover specialists. That was when merger mania got into full swing.

Saatchi & Saatchi, of England, almost singlehandedly created the tidal wave. It was respected as a small, aggressive, creative agency before it started on the acquisition trail. Its biggest coup came in 1979 when it helped Margaret Thatcher become Britain's prime minister. Now, a little more than ten years later, it is reportedly Number Two in the world with billings in the neighbourhood of four billion dollars. Whether it is still highly creative is another matter entirely.

In a classroom I could make a good case for the megaagency. I could argue that bigness gives an advertising agency greater depth, more talent, more services to offer clients. In reality, the story is quite different. You always have one person who is the link between the client and the agency. That person is either the account manager or the account executive: the "suits" as they're referred to in the business, although that should be changed to "suits and skirts", since more and more women are now acting in that capacity.

The job of the account executive is to consult with clients and to communicate their needs and desires back to the agency. It is an important function obviously, because, without adequate information, you cannot produce effective advertising. It is also efficient since everybody knows who is responsible for client relations. That means any question that crops up in the agency, you know who the contact is, whether it be a query on creative, media, research, or billings.

In a mega-agency, the line of communications begins to blur. You may still have only one account manager; but, because your own agency staff has doubled or even quadrupled, your internal communications begin to become a nightmare. No longer is it a simple team effort, but a bureaucratic jungle that the account executive must wade through in order to deliver what the client wants.

In major manufacturing companies (i.e., packaged goods), the marketing of each product line is broken down into separate departments. That works because each marketing manager is responsible only for his or her specific line. Indeed, different managers within the same company may be fighting with each other for the same consumer dollar. Will you buy peanut butter or jam? But they don't have to worry about any other aspect of the production and distribution of the product. That is the responsibility of other management resources.

At the ad-agency level, however, such segmentation of responsibility is a drawback. You must have complete interdepartmental co-operation in your marketing efforts if you are to succeed. Advertising demands it. After all, you are performing a number of vital services on behalf of a single client. And much of what each group does is directed toward a single end, the marketing of the product itself. You may even be advertising a number of separate product lines for the same company. Such co-operation within an agency involves not only the ads themselves, but where you place them, how you research the market, how you maintain the corporate identity. That demands, not a dispersal of responsibilities, but a cohesive team effort.

The larger the agency gets, the less the chances are of achieving a proficient team effort on behalf of the client. Most of the agency's internal energies become directed to its own fiscal health instead of that of the client. The people who affected the merger — or mergers — are in charge of making it work.

The administrative staff, which wouldn't know a good ad if it tripped over one, begins to grow disproportionately to meet the demands of accountancy. Before you know it, there are more rules and procedures before you can begin to get creative, more paper flying around that has nothing to do with the true business at hand. And more internal wrangling. The business side, justifiably concerned about profit and loss, unfortunately begins to dominate all other areas of the business; and it does so in a dictatorial, disruptive manner.

The result all too often is that the real ad people begin to take the line of least resistance. "A good ad is a sold ad." Why try to be truly creative — a process that cannot be dictated by time allotment — when what management wants are the commissions generated by the advertising? In other words, what you get is production-line advertising: dull, unimaginative, safe, uninspired — but profitable. Not only does conservatism take hold of the creative department, it infiltrates media buying, research, production, and every other area that makes an agency operate effectively, if not always efficiently. You need efficiency if you are going to pay your bills and show a profit. But good advertising cannot be dictated by a time clock, does not have a simple formula that allows you to blend ingredients at will, cannot be packaged as if it were mass produced.

Eventually, in mega-agencies, the five cornerstones of good advertising begin to erode. *Originality* is generally the first to disappear. With it, inevitably, go *style* and *artistry*. Then, sadly enough, I believe *integrity* and *honesty* are worn down because nobody in the agency truly understands — or gives a damn — about what the hell the product is or how it should be sold. Just get it out of the shop as quickly and profitably as possible. As Bill Bernbach once said succinctly: "The truth isn't the truth until they believe you; and they can't believe you if they don't know what you're saying; and they can't know what you're saying if they don't listen to you; and they won't listen to you if you're not interesting. And you won't be interesting unless you say things freshly, originally, and imaginatively."

Production-line advertising based solely on the agency's bottom line does not even come close to meeting Bill's requirements. And that is why so much of it today is so boring, so infantile, so insensitive to both the client and the consumer.

Another facet of the mega-agency syndrome makes it virtually irreconcilable with good advertising. In most product lines, there are generally only a limited number of giants. In cars, for instance, you have the American Big Three: GM, Ford, and Chrysler. Then the Japanese: Toyota, Honda, Nissan, Suzuki, Mazda, and Subaru. And the Koreans: Hyundai. In Europe: Volkswagen, Fiat, Volvo, Saab, and Renault. They're the most popular cars and they total fifteen.

A mega-agency, because of inherent conflicts of interest, can only represent — at best — one automobile company at a time. The automotive accounts are spread out. The same is true for all other fields of endeavour where large advertising expenditures are required to move product. That means any agency is automatically limited in the number of big individual accounts it can get its hands on. At the same time, there are thousands of other potential clients, operating on a lesser scale, but with largish advertising budgets. If each mega-agency has one major account in a number of non-conflicting fields, it is obvious it is going to spend most of its time — and talent — on those accounts. It must protect them by every means possible because it is so dependent upon them. But it needs the other, smaller clients as well to augment its gross revenues — to grow. Otherwise it becomes stagnant.

Now comes the ultimate question. How would you like to be a second-tier client in such an agency? And that's the incontestable problem with mega-agencies. They grew out of mergers and the acquisition of major accounts. Although those clients may be served relatively well, other lesser ones are relegated to second-class status.

Then there is the takeover of national manufacturing companies by international conglomerates. We, in Canada, have had lots of experience with that. What happens then, generally, is that the multinational decides the marketing should be done by the subsidiary advertising agency of its home-based mega-agency. Another account goes foreign, another piece of business is lost. Merger mania feeds on merger mania. All, however, is not lost. A backlash is occurring. Corporate marketing people are not stupid. The mega-agencies may be able to dance and weave for a time; but, eventually, they cannot cover their inadequacies when it gets down to solid advertising results. That is the real reason there is so much so-called lifestyle advertising around. It is intended to keep clients happy. The bigger the campaign, the glitzier it is, the more time the mega-agency can buy. We are all human, after all, and slice-of-life ads do look good. In the long run, however, they mainly fail to make the required impact. At some point the client says: "Wait a minute. What the hell are we doing?" Then all hell breaks loose — and it's happening.

Two emerging trends are apparent in advertising. The first is that many good advertising people are getting fed up with the pressure-cooker, structured environment of the big agencies. They are leaving and either setting themselves up as freelancers or, in combination with others, setting up small boutiques. They are not selling jewellery or fashionable clothes. A "boutique" is a small shop that concentrates on certain areas of advertising. It may be creative alone, or it may be a combination of creative and account management. It may specialize in media buys, or research, or direct marketing. What it does is offer clients specialized services. And if it doesn't have one required service, it works together with another boutique or with freelance help. The vast majority of these people are accepted professionals. They have good track records. And all they want to do is perform in the best way possible.

These boutiques originally became fashionable in the late sixties and early seventies. Most then were based on the fact that the people who started them were ambitious. They wanted to build their own agencies, beginning with their own recognized talents. Some succeeded, others did not. Now, however, the style appears to have changed. Starting up a new agency with full services is not the boutique's primary concern. What they want to do is work at their own particular craft, using their own particular skills to fill the void left in the marketplace. Quality and personal commitment to an account is what they offer. As Sam Slick said, "A small house well filled is better than an empty palace."

It is working, and that is trend Number Two. In the past year or so, a number of large advertisers have given substantial slices of their ad business to these new entrepreneurs, both in Canada and the U.S.: contracts in the millions of dollars. I don't want to name even a few because I don't know how successful each will be. And I certainly don't want the mega-agency people reading this book and saying: "Gee! Goodis named this boutique and look what happened? They bombed." I'm not going to help the big boys save their own bacon. I have no trouble naming a few excellent freelance copywriters and art directors who have left the Canadian agency ranks and are doing well on their own, such as Martin Keen, Steve Catlin, Dean Bradley, Bill Edwards, and Harrison Yates. All extremely talented, and each a specialist in his own right.

This doesn't mean that the mega-agencies see the handwriting on the wall. Unfortunately, no; although a number reportedly are having serious financial problems, including Saatchi & Saatchi. What it does point to, though, is a long overdue rethinking of the role of the agency with regard to both clients and consumers. Perhaps, as in the Eastern Bloc countries, this will lead to greater freedom in the areas that count the most, and a withering of stifling bureaucracy. As I have consistently said, I am against the commission system in advertising. It may have worked once but it is an anachronism now. With multi-media campaigns and ever-increasing expenditures to cover the cost of them, fixed commissions are just too big a temptation to an agency to pad the budget. And it doesn't have to do it in order to cheat the client outright. All it has to do is rationalize its advertising recommendations on the basis that it wants to make sure there is enough weight and strength to the campaign to be successful, or that it needs to cover all the bases in order to reach as many potential consumers as possible. When you are dealing with multi-million-dollar accounts, what is a few more million to make absolutely sure you are achieving maximum impact? At fifteen per cent commission, a hell of a lot of profit.

That may be an overly negative view. The ad business, after all, is not made up of crooks. It does, however, highlight the dilemma. Budgets are not necessarily structured on getting the maximum return for an optimum output. More often than not, they are designed on the basis of a maximum expenditure to get a suitable result. And once you have had an account for a number of years, the rationalization for budget increases comes more easily, more naturally. After all, the figures prove it. The only problem is that the figures are often based on projections of presumed needs rather than on hard evidence.

Hard data is not easy to come by in advertising. Such guidelines as how many consumers you reach and with what frequency you reach them are based on the average number of viewers, listeners, and readers there are in the various media. Even the type of consumer (young or old, female or male, affluent or not) you reach is based on periodic studies, not hard data. A male more than eighteen years of age may watch television, on average, twenty-two and a half hours per week. That is what the research shows. Supposedly, for a woman in the same age category it is twenty-six and a half hours. But the data cannot guarantee that. There are just too many variables.

Advertising is by no means an exact science. It is half art, half business. It stands to reason that budgeting is not an exact science either. That is why I prefer the fee system to one with built-in commissions. You establish your fees on the basis of the work to be done on behalf of a client. You can calculate your internal costs. Your external costs, be they production or media expenditures, are based on what you believe the client requires to get the job done. Under such a system, you do not go around throwing money at a problem simply because there is a profit in it for yourself, but because you believe that is the required amount to solve it.

A new trend may be a compensation system for agencies, based on fees commensurate with how well the client's products sell. In other words, market performance by the company will determine how much of a fee — above a base — the agency receives. The concrete results the agency produces will determine its revenues — and its profits. That could be exciting, and require a cohesive team effort in order to be successful. Maybe we should call it a "success bonus".

It might also broaden the base of operations for agencies,

since the company might be doing promotion, direct marketing, and public relations, as well as advertising. The only way to judge the effectiveness of the whole operation would be to have it under one roof. Otherwise, too many agencies might be — justifiably or not — claiming credit for the company's sales record for any particular year. It would also force such agencies to balance their approach to the marketplace rather than throwing the majority of the budget at high-cost media expenditures. What is best for the client would be the new approach; or, rather, a return to the old approach. Let the battle begin. Then we will see if the mega-agencies can really compete. And survive.

The jury is out.

CHAPTER
TEN

Vote as You Like,
But Vote Liberal

I love politics. As a matter of fact, just about as much as I love women, but not as much as I love my family. However, I've given my love and support to more than one wife, but only to one political party. That's the Liberal Party of Canada.

I became involved in the political scene a couple of years after I opened my first agency. The person who introduced me to it was Martin Goldfarb who owns one of the most successful public opinion research firms in Canada and, at that time, the Liberal Party's longtime pollster.

My first political convention was an exciting one, not only for me, but for the Party because it was so hotly contested. That was in 1968. Prime Minister Lester B. Pearson was stepping down. Many of his senior cabinet ministers were striving to replace him. I was involved in the Paul Hellyer campaign, mainly as a neophyte communications adviser.

Of course, everyone knows that Pierre Elliott Trudeau, Pearson's personal choice for leader, won on the fourth ballot. And Paul Hellyer never again became a significant force in the federal political scene. I might have had a finger in that, unwittingly. His major speech to the delegates at the convention was largely my handiwork. It was a disaster. Paul's style and mine were not even close, yet I tried to force my personality onto him. I learned very quickly you cannot do that — at his expense, unfortunately.

It was not the auspicious entry I would have planned for myself, but I became fascinated with the process. I also met Senator Keith Davey, the mastermind behind the ensuing Trudeau election campaigns. Keith and I hit it off from the beginning. He introduced me to the new PM, which took all of three seconds. I had no idea that, only a couple of years later, I would become one of his close advisers, and that Keith would become one of my dearest friends.

My interest in politics — indeed, my interest in advertising — stems from my youth. I was the youngest of four children. As such, my father, Louis, took me almost everywhere he went. And the places he visited, the events he attended, made a strong impression on me. He was a trade union organizer (one of the founders of the now defunct Labour League) and a left-wing socialist. That meant I ended up at a lot of union hall meetings, rallies, and even on picket lines. Since this was the mid-thirties, the labor movement was in constant flux, fighting within itself just as much as it fought the factory owners in Toronto's seedy garment district.

The philosophy meant little to me at the time because I was just a kid in short pants. What fascinated me was the effect public speakers had on their audiences. It could be negative, it could be positive. What enthralled me was how vocal and violent those reactions were. A single person could speak for only a few brief moments and all hell would break loose. The power of words, the power of persuasion. That's what captured my attention.

I remember vividly the first time I was in Maple Leaf Gardens. I was perhaps five or six. There must have been fifteen thousand people there. It was a rally to raise funds for the Republican side in the Spanish Civil War and recruits for the Mackenzie-Papineau Battalion, the Canadian contingent that was being organized to fight against the Fascist insurgent Generalissimo Franco in Spain. Speaker after speaker came to the podium and exhorted the crowd. And time after time it reacted with thunderous applause and with standing, flag-waving ovations. I could feel that emotion surge right through me. I didn't even know where Spain was. I applauded and cheered along with everyone else. As each new speaker rose and spoke into the microphone, there would be almost complete silence. Then a crescendo of noise. The power those people appeared to have made an indelible impression upon me.

I believe that is why I love making speeches to this day; some twenty a year. I get to say what I want to say, the audience gets to react. And I always try to challenge an audience as well as entertain it. That gives me a high that is almost impossible to describe. Don't take me wrong. I respect my audiences but I must get a reaction from them or I consider it a wasted effort.

My father, Louis Goodis, died when I was seven. It was a monumental loss to me. Slowly but surely I began to learn and espouse his socialist beliefs. But just as surely, times began to change and so did I. Along with many of my political beliefs. I make no apologies for my left-wing upbringing (as if I had a choice in the matter). It taught me a unique way of looking at the world. As I told author Erna Paris for her excellent book on the Jewish experience in Canada: "If my father could see me now, he might turn over in his grave. But more likely he would have a little smile on his face. He'd say: 'It was a nice idea (socialism) but now that things have changed, go do what you have to do.' Why the hell should I feel guilty? I gave the ideology a hell of a shot. I gave them my whole youth. It didn't work. Now I have set my hand to something else."

The other impressionable experience of my youth came in the early fifties when I helped form The Travellers, a vocal group that specialized in folk songs. We became popular in Canada during those few brief years, even made a number

The Travellers — Canada's most highly acclaimed folk-song group.

of records for Columbia. But it was the live audience concerts that reinforced my belief in the power of words, in the emotions they can evoke.

The Travellers sang songs in about twelve different languages. It was my job to introduce them with a few words about that language and an explanation of the background surrounding the melody and the lyrics. Because it was a time of political protest — and we all still had strong convictions in that regard — many of the tunes had revolutionary themes. Nevertheless, we recognized the fact that we couldn't be political all of the time. So we sang other tunes as well, many of which were humorous.

Mixing and matching these elements was a challenge so we could retain our audience. I enjoyed it, not simply because of the popularity we achieved, but because I learned how to woo audiences with conviction and win them with humour. That experience was a major lesson for me when I entered advertising; again when I got involved in politics. It was, I guess you could say, my bridge into mass communications.

The most popular folk group in North America at that time was The Weavers. We were on the same stage with them a number of times, enjoyed their company, even exchanged songs from time to time. Unlike that group, however, we were fortunate. In Canada, we didn't have anything like the ugly McCarthy hearings in the U.S. Senator Joe McCarthy, who spearheaded a vendetta against the left wing, pronounced The Weavers to be Communists and they were blacklisted from the entertainment world. That was the end for them. It also taught me my own lesson. Half-truths are a deception, no matter how sincerely they're uttered. And eventually, you'll be found out, as McCarthy was. He ended up on the junk pile of American history. So you don't play around with half-truths. That held me in good stead in both advertising and politics.

Why the Liberal Party accepted me as an adviser must be a mystery to some of them. Just before Expo '67 opened in Montreal, I delivered a speech in Toronto in which I accused Lester B. Pearson's government of porkbarrel politics. I angrily detailed how all the federal advertising, the construction of its exhibits, even the production of the literature, was going to agencies and companies closely associated with the Party.

The speech got a lot of press. I was pleased that I had stirred things up because my agency wasn't getting any of the Expo work. What I didn't know — but Keith Davey explained to me a couple of years later — was that the then Secretary of State, Judy LaMarsh, was infuriated with me. She wanted to sue. The Cabinet decided the wiser choice was to simply let the storm blow through, which, of course, it did. But a lot of Liberals had my name etched in their minds as a troublemaker who should be avoided at all costs. Nevertheless, I was invited to join the advertising team that was to plot the strategy for the 1974 general election, Trudeau's first as PM. It was my inauguration into election advertising.

HOMMAGES À MONSIEUR JERRY GOODIS, CONFÉRENCIER
À L'OCCASION DU DÉJEUNER-CAUSERIE DU PUBLICITÉ-CLUB DE MONTRÉAL,
AU CHÂTEAU CHAMPLAIN, LE 23 SEPTEMBRE 1970.

1974 election victory party at prime minister's residence with national election staff. Jerry Goodis is standing in the front row.

Keith Davey essentially mapped out the strategy. We became the tacticians. He would outline to us the Party's platform and those points in it that were considered to be the more significant. Under the chairmanship of Jerry Grafstein, a lawyer and now a senator, a select group of senior ad people would attempt to capitalize on that strategy, that platform. The major agency players were Terry O'Malley, of Vickers & Benson, Hank Karpus, of Ronalds-Reynolds, George Elliott, of MacLaren, and myself.

During my experiences from 1972 until 1984, when Pierre Elliott Trudeau stepped down as leader of the Party, the semi-weekly — often daily — advertising meetings were attended by no more than six or seven people. They were held, of course, only during that period encompassing an election campaign; although, through Keith, we all kept in touch during the interim periods. What fascinated me about them from the beginning was the fact that decisions were always a matter of consensus. That may seem strange since the three or four advertising agencies that made up the bulk of the committee were normally at each other's throats when they went back to the marketplace. Yet it worked remarkably well.

That didn't mean there were no underlying tensions. For example, Keith thought Terry O'Malley was the Moses of Canadian copywriting. I never agreed with that. In the first place, Moses was an account executive, not a copywriter. Secondly, like a number of the ten commandments Moses brought down from the mountain, I thought Terry often had a tendency to overwrite, both in headlines and in copy. On the other hand, I had great respect for the intuitive skills of Hank Karpus and George Elliott, with whom I was later to work at MacLaren. While their styles were different from mine, we were more closely attuned. Therefore, sometimes I had to bite my tongue when Terry made a presentation. It wasn't that the ideas weren't discussed openly. What I had to learn was to be more judicious in my comments.

Once Keith had outlined the platform, we simply went away and came back with creative concepts we thought would work. Then, after a free exchange on those ideas, decisions would be made. From time to time, depending on the agenda, Keith would attend, perhaps even someone from the Prime Minister's Office like Jim Coutts, Trudeau's principal secretary. From the outset, I loved the experience, the interchange of ideas, even the tensions. Once the creative approach had been decided upon, the work would be divided among the agencies according to their accepted strengths (television, radio, print, signage). At first I took on the free-time political broadcasts since our agency was by far the smallest. Later, when I moved to MacLaren, my role changed substantially. Because MacLaren was the agency originally chosen by Walter Gordon, Keith Davey, and Lester Pearson to help breath new life into the Liberal Party, it was always viewed as the dominant force at "Red Leaf", followed by Vickers & Benson. I became far more active and influential, drawing closer to the Prime Minister, the Cabinet, and Keith Davey — even when elections were not in the offing. Being Vice-Chairman of MacLaren endowed me with a kind of metaphysical mantel, I guess. I was "legitimized", so to speak. Mother Mac was a dominant force in Canadian — and Liberal — advertising, but Red Leaf Communications Ltd. was the entity under which all media selections were made during an election. It was also the billing agency so that better control over costs could be maintained. It worked, despite the fact that some journalists, from time to time, liked to give it a pernicious character, as if it were a secret society or a subversive movement.

My role in Liberal election campaigning shouldn't be overblown. Although it was a vital function to the party, one has to remember this. There were only four elections during that decade and a half. The Liberals won three and lost one. It wasn't a full-time job. At the same time, when we met, the pressures were intense. Our whole lives were focussed on those committee meetings and the work that evolved from them. It was an immense burden for all of us — and we loved it. I look back on those times with both joy and pride.

The sessions revolved around the ever-increasing pace of the election. How could we capitalize on the platform creatively and convincingly? Where should we spend our budget? When should we spend most of it? What was the opposition doing? How was the public reacting, according to Goldfarb's public opinion polls? They were exhilarating times. At the same time, pressure-packed. It was as if every few years, you decided to take off on your yacht and explore new waters, with all the preparation, excitement, perils, and enjoyment you could derive from it.

In order for me to produce the free-time broadcasts in 1972 I needed the co-operation of the Prime Minister. After all, he was featured in most of them. In order to discuss the subject in depth, Keith and I arranged to go out to 24 Sussex Drive. I was nervous. Keith warned me that, whatever I did, I was not to sit in the dining room chair closest to the north window when we were invited to sit down to lunch. According to him, there was a hotline phone underneath that particular chair, and only the Prime Minister sat there. I said I would remember.

We had an excellent session in Trudeau's study and, as expected, he asked us to stay to lunch. We were still conferring when we entered the dining room. He waved his hand, beckoning us to sit. I was so engrossed in the conversation I took the first chair closest to me. Needless to say, it was the one with the phone under it. I knew I had made a blunder instantly because Keith's eyes popped out of his head and his mouth fell open. I was about to rise when the Prime Minister waved me back into the chair. "That's all right, Jerry" he said. "When the phone rings just pick it up. If it's a girl, hang up. Otherwise I'll take it."

I felt like a fool, but he allowed me to sit there all through lunch. I was petrified the phone would ring. Keith was in stitches, and the Prime Minister simply continued his comments. It was probably the most embarrassing lunch I have ever sat through. At the same time, it highlighted two engaging attributes of Pierre Trudeau's personality, of which I was to see a lot more of as we became closer. The first, obviously, was his quick wit. The second was the fact that, even though I was a young, political upstart, he treated me in a most courteous and considerate manner and not as many presidents of companies I've known would have done. The Prime Minister just wanted me to feel comfortable. And I did.

I found through all my associations with him that he truly loves Canada and its people. He cares for them individually, and he cares for them collectively. The latter, I believe, can be seen in what he tried to do for the country, both as a justice minister and as PM. To some that may sound like political fodder. I don't think so. I think his record on behalf of the country proves it. I can remember a number of occasions when he phoned me in Toronto simply to discuss my thoughts on some problem that was bothering him. It was not that he thought I was a pundit. It was simply that he was continually seeking input from a wide array of people when a particular situation arose where he thought their advice might be appropriate. Once he phoned to solicit my opinion on whether Canada should move its embassy in Israel from Tel Aviv to Jerusalem. What others thought was important to him. By the way, I was opposed to such a move, unlike most leaders of the Jewish community.

He showed the same concern for individuals. Once I had to be in Ottawa the same day as my daughter Leslie's birthday. The Prime Minister, Keith Davey, and I were travelling from Sussex Drive to the House of Commons in the PM's limousine. Keith mentioned the fact of her birthday. Immediately, the Prime Minister asked his driver to turn around and return home. He dashed out of the car, came back a few moments later and handed me a handwritten note on his stationery. It was addressed to Leslie and it said, "Leslie: A million congratulations on your birthday. Sorry to have your father in Ottawa." When I got home, she was thrilled with the note. Understandably, I was deeply taken by his thought-fulness.

However, he didn't suffer fools gladly (as the bishop said to the actress). He had a built-in bullshit detector. On a couple of occasions when I first began to counsel him, he would ask how a speech of his had gone, or an interview. If it had gone badly, I'd hum and hah, trying to avoid a direct answer. He'd just stare at me, stare me down. I learned quickly that what he wanted was the truth. From then on, I gave it to him. He not only accepted it, but was appreciative. He didn't like making speeches or being interviewed. He was an exceedingly shy man, but he wanted to do the job as best he could. And he wanted the straight goods from his advisers so he could improve.

He was also tolerant, even when I embarrassed him which is what happened when I was introduced to Queen Elizabeth II. It was at the Commonwealth Games in Edmonton. The Prime Minister's Office kindly invited my wife and me to the opening ceremonies and, later, to meet Her Majesty.

The protocol when you meet the Queen is that you do not ever shake hands with her, nor speak to her until she speaks to you. Guess what? Out of instinct, combined with some nervousness, I stuck out my hand when the Prime Minister introduced me. On his part, he rolled his eyes in exasperation. I also made some remark to her, like what a pleasure it was to meet her. She didn't even flinch. She shook my hand and responded kindly to whatever I said. As she moved on down the line, the Prime Minister gave me a look as if to say: "I can't take you anywhere, Jerry." Needless to say, I was embarrassed and took a good deal of kidding from others in attendance.

The second episode requires a little background. I was in Israel on holiday with my family just after the Liberals had won a general election. If memory serves me correctly, it was 1974. I had worked hard on the campaign. My family agreed that we all deserved the trip.

Then I got a phone call in Jerusalem from Keith Davey. There was going to be a celebration, a victory party, a "roast" of the Prime Minister at 24 Sussex Drive in a few days and, according to him, I *had* to be there. I protested, but he insisted. I flew back to Ottawa via Amsterdam, leaving my family to continue on their holiday.

When I arrived in Ottawa I was suffering from a severe case of jet lag. Nevertheless, I went to the roast, but with no intention of getting involved in the fun other than to make a few, I hoped, humorous remarks. When all the participants had finished giving it to the Prime Minister, he rose and, one by one, got his own back.

It came my turn. He informed the gathering that, a year or so earlier, when the two of us were leaving his residence to attend a meeting elsewhere, he stopped at the door and told me to go ahead. Supposedly, he'd forgotten to take something with him. When I walked out under the portico, his RCMP honour guard saluted. Then he appeared and it saluted again. What he didn't tell me at the time, but he was happy to tell this gathering, was that he had snuck away earlier from our meeting and told the honour guard: "Don't forget to salute the little guy."

I know when he told that story I went every colour of the rainbow. The reason was that I remembered the occasion vividly. I also recalled, just as vividly, what a nice feeling it was to be saluted. I had no idea that he had set me up. And, rather than joshing me about it at the time, he had patiently waited for a more appropriate — and public — occasion. It took me all of ten seconds to forgive him. How can you dislike anyone with that kind of impeccable timing?

I can't claim that Pierre Elliott Trudeau and I became close social friends. That would be an overstatement. He did treat me as a valued associate when we worked together and, above all, took an engaging and thoughtful interest in my personal and family life. You can't ask much more, even from your closest friend.

One of the perks of becoming involved in politics, especially if you are on the winning side, is that you get invitations to special events, often historical, and the opportunity to meet interesting people. You can also be asked to perform certain tasks or favours, which, although intriguing, can also be draining.

Once I was asked to deliver a diplomatic pouch to U Thant when he was Secretary-General of the United Nations. To this day I have no idea why it didn't go through normal diplomatic channels, or why I was chosen as the messenger. All I was asked to do was to fly to New York, deliver the communiqué, wait for an answer, and fly back to Ottawa.

'WILL THE REAL JERRY GOODIS STAND UP.'

Globe and Mail *Editorial-page cartoon featuring the leader of the Ontario Liberal Party during an election campaign purportedly being manipulated by Jerry Goodis.*

I was not used to this cloak-and-dagger stuff. When I arrived in New York, I took a cab to the UN and introduced myself at the main reception area. Within seconds I was being escorted up to the Secretary-General's office. When I met him, he was exceedingly gracious and asked that I sit across the desk from him while he read the communiqué. The only other person in the room was an assistant with whom he discussed — in muted tones — the message.

This was during the time of the Viet Nam War. Whether my trip had anything to do with that I'll probably never know. What I do remember is that, when the reply was being prepared, he talked to me as if we were close associates. At one point, he got onto the topic of war itself. I was astounded he was even discussing it. I was also startled at the emotion he showed during that part of the conversation. His major point was that here he was living in a country as head of the UN and that same country was "raping" the land of his neighbours. That was the word he used, rape.

I had no idea what to say; so, for a change, I remained silent. When the response was ready, he gave it to me and shook my hand. Then I was escorted back to the main entrance. The whole visit had lasted a little more than an hour, but I was exhausted. The intensity with which the Secretary-General had spoken of the war in Viet Nam was beyond my experience. I hadn't expected it. I was shaking from the experience.

This was not the kind of experience to which an ad man is accustomed. I was out of my league and I knew it. It took every ounce of energy just to make sure I didn't leave the response to the communiqué in a cab or on the plane. I scanned the newspapers for days afterwards to see if anything was reported that I could relate to the visit. There was nothing. A short time later U Thant died of cancer. During my visit, he probably knew he had the disease. Perhaps that was why he became so emotional during our meeting. But I will never know whether that was true either.

Another nerve-wracking episode occurred during the period of the October Crisis in Canada when the FLQ kidnapped a British diplomat and murdered a Quebec cabinet minister. I was almost a weekly visitor to the capital. It wasn't that I was involved as an adviser. I was, however, doing a fair amount of work for various government departments, and came to understand the monumental pressures and tensions involved in such a national crisis. I also became aware of how well politicians respond under such trying conditions. We may be able to accuse them of a lot of things, but lack of courage in crises is not one of them. I was amazed at how calm they were, especially the cabinet ministers with whom I came in contact.

At one point I had a meeting with Labour Minister Bryce Mackasey, who was then the Minister of Labour. We were to discuss an advertising campaign to do with discrimination in hiring practices. We had just gotten into the subject when he received a phone call. He told me he had an emergency Cabinet meeting in five minutes. I was to wait for him in his office and watch the World Series on television. He'd be back once the meeting had ended.

When he returned, the first thing he asked was what the score in the game was. Then he sat down at his desk and explained to me that Cabinet had just decided to ask Parliament to invoke the War Measures Act. I simply sat there, aghast. What the hell were they doing? Was the country really coming to this? I knew Bryce well. I couldn't understand why he wasn't as shaken — and incensed — as I was. He simply sat there waiting for a reaction. Finally, when I was about to erupt, he simply put up a hand. "Jerry," he said "it has to be done. Now let's get back to what we were talking about." His calmness prevailed. We began discussing discrimination in the workplace.

Until the crisis was over, every time I went somewhere in Ottawa with a high official, we were accompanied in the car by a member of the armed forces with a submachine gun sitting on his lap. It never seemed to bother any of the people I was with, but it shook the stuffing out of me. I never became used to it. They just seemed to take it in stride. I give them credit. The business of the government continued as if nothing else was going on. In my estimation, that took guts. It made me see politicians and public servants in a whole new light.

One of the key elements in any election campaign, as far as advertising is concerned, is the theme you are going to develop around the party's platform. On what visions of the country are you going to focus your efforts? That is undoubtedly the most difficult task, which is why you have to gather around you diverse talent. Only thus can you elicit the creative thinking that eventually provides you with a single concept that has the required appeal and impact.

An election theme must encompass a great many ideas. Although it is an umbrella covering many themes, of necessity, it must also be cohesive. And, above all, it must say something to individual voters. It is the glue that binds all of the ways you promote the party and what it stands for.

The news media, of course, have a field day with any election theme. It is generally one of the first elements that surfaces after the election is called. Having little else to write about, reporters jump on it. Then the columnists and commentators have a go, making as much fun of it as they can, twisting it. That is because the press has no idea of a theme's importance in winning voters to your party, or the depth of thinking that normally goes into it. Journalists believe we ad types want to sell the party as if it were soap. Nonsense. Advertising is only one facet of any campaign and we all know it. How important it is is difficult to measure. There has never been a successful political party in modern times that didn't advertise in an election.

At the same time, a significant number of press pundits have placed the blame for a dismal showing on the very same advertising process they so often blissfully dismiss as redundant and unimportant. They like to have it both ways. One of the best examples of this double-standard occurred after the 1972 election. The Liberal theme was "The Land Is Strong." The media blamed the poor results of the party on the theme. And the person who was lambasted the most was MacLaren Vice-President George Elliott, who purportedly invented it. He was crucified in the media. If it's reported in newspapers, on TV and radio, then it must be true. That is another fallacy we must live with. George denied to me ever having had anything to do with it. And I believe him.

I believed him; first, because, when he told me, he was outraged to the point of tears at having to carry the burden for something to which he was opposed. Secondly, I've asked people in the Party who were active then and they verify what George said to me. However, no one wants to admit who invented it. The closest I can get is that a high-ranking Liberal politician wrote it and insisted on its being used. I realize that is not hard evidence, but neither is the fact George got the blame simply because he was involved in the advertising during that election. Bum rap, and George took it well. I could not have.

From my own point of view, it was a vacuous theme. It didn't centre on the Liberal platform. It didn't sum up the Party's intentions if elected. It was pap: words the electorate could easily dismiss because it told them nothing. It could have been said at almost any period in this country's history. As well, it held out little incentive for them to vote Liberal.

I have taken my fair share of flack during elections, too. I have been quoted in the media as defending the advertising during the Trudeau campaigns: "Why is it immoral to sell a politician? Everybody sells something. Sure you try to emphasize the candidate's strong points. Why not? When you're chasing a girl, you don't tell her you've got bad breath." I have no problem with that statement, even today. Advertising is selling. But you don't sell politicians in the same way you sell soap. That is what the news media cannot seem to get through their cumulative, interfering heads.

When you attempt to convince people to support a charitable cause, such as cancer or diabetes, you don't devise ads for it in the same way as you would for a consumer product. It would be stupid and insensitive. And the same holds true for election advertising. One of the columnists who used my quote on "selling" politicians — and used it out of context — was Allan Fotheringham, of *Maclean's*. In the same column he described me as an "aging flack with a paste-over hairstyle." Well, whoopee. That gives you a perceptive view of my talents as an ad man. He also summed me up this way: "Goodis is a good flack, a good shill. That means he would spike his mother sliding into second base. The Liberals hire only the best. If you're going to buy a huckster, go to the top." What glib, supercilious crap. I far more prefer advertising people who sell soap than the views of columnists like Fotheringham, who attempt only to build a reputation for themselves at the expense of others. And, besides that, he's never even met me. How does he know what I'm like? Did he know that my mother was dying of cancer when he wrote that? Would it have mattered? The anomaly of the news media with regard to politics and politicians is that they so often take certain events (frequently insignificant) or idiosyncrasies (frequently physical) and twist them to their own designs. They then try to convince the public that they are of monumental importance.

Trudeaumania swept the country in the late sixties and early seventies. The so-called ad hucksters did not invent the phrase, the press did. It was said that Trudeau was young, which he wasn't. They said he was a public charmer when, as I said earlier, he was an extremely shy and private person. One of the "great" events that gave credence to this media legend of Trudeaumania was the fact that he was photographed jackknifing into a swimming pool while campaigning. To the press that proved he was a renaissance man, capable of accomplishing almost anything. The photo got not just national but international coverage. How could you not love a leader who performed such feats? Was this an advertising or public relations ploy? It was media hype, nothing less. And they know it, the supercilious clowns.

A few years later, we contracted Trudeauphobia when a significant number of the media became disenchanted with him. That was another invention of the fourth estate, another bias that was developed to skew the national perspective on him. And there were examples within the Progressive Conservative ranks as well. Robert Stanfield once fumbled a football tossed to him, and was thereafter relegated by certain sectors of the media as an incompetent leader. Joe Clark because of a receding chin and stilted speech, came to be called "Joe Who." Both men were leaders of their party. Both were maligned by the news media unsparingly even though each undoubtedly had more intelligence and leadership ability than any of the reporters who covered them.

There is an old joke about Joe Clark when he was Prime Minister. He was showing the press around his home and its grounds. During the tour, he was accompanied by his dog. Inevitably, one of the reporters asked him if his dog could do any tricks. The PM picked up a stick and threw it out onto a pond. The dog didn't swim out to retrieve it, it walked on top of the water. The next day's headlines across the nation were: "Joe Clark's dog can't swim."

That's the type of thing the press does all the time. It portrays public figures as it wishes them to be seen, not as they are. It may build one up and tear another down. And it has the nerve to then call advertising people who are politically committed nothing but "shills" and "hucksters". Well, no matter how hard they try to sell that guff, it just doesn't wash. They're the camp followers, not us. And, like I said, they know it.

One of the unpleasant components of political party advertising is the fact that, in an election, there is only one winner; the party that gains power. Such a statement may appear to be self-evident; but one that you had better adapt to quickly if you are going to survive in the political arena. In normal product advertising, if you gain a bigger share of the market, your client is happy. You're happy. In politics, the only share is the whole pie. Otherwise, there are a lot of unhappy people whom you must face. And they do not take too kindly to you. It's the age-old shoot-the-messenger syndrome. There is not only the pressure to produce, but the pressure to win.

The ultimate task confronting you is to try to provide a campaign that bridges the gap between the politicians and the electorate. You may say that is overly cynical, but it is true. Not everyone loves the party candidate nominated in each riding. Not every candidate will be able to speak lucidly about what the party will do if elected. Not every candidate even follows the party policy. Therefore, the task of advertising is to smooth over the rough edges so the people will vote for as many of your candidates across the country, regardless of their perceived gifts or inadequacies.

If you have a dynamic leader, as Pierre Trudeau was, the task is far simpler than if the opposite is true. You have a flagbearer who epitomizes party policy, a person who has appealing attributes. It is someone whom the public feels it can trust. The leader of the party and the theme of the campaign become as one.

If you do not have such a leader, then your task is far more difficult. In certain cases, it is even better to downplay his or her role and put your emphasis on the strength of the party as a whole. Joe Clark, even though he won one election, did not show the required presence of leadership to continue winning. John Turner fell short as well. With Brian Mulroney, it is an on-again, off-again thing. It is not whether their leadership is adequate or not, it is whether they can project themselves to the electorate adequately. The press loves to call it "charisma". What it really is is comparison shopping; and, nowadays, it's mainly done through that screen in your living room.

In campaign-planning, you must first find out what the gut issues are in the public mind. That takes in-depth research. What do people really want out of their government? What are their major concerns heading into an election? These aren't the public opinion polls sponsored by the media and foisted upon us almost daily. That is only a transient reaction to a particular question at one particular time. And, like the weather, it can change within hours. What we are really talking about is tracking vital questions over a considerable period of time. That reflects, not just a simple breakdown of attitudes, but trends in people's thinking. Are they moving one way, or another? Why are they moving?

Most politicians deny that they pay any attention to polling. They are correct because the individual polls by themselves are insignificant. It is the trend that is reflected in them over a period of time that tells the tale. What did people think three years ago about a certain issue? Did it change the year after, or the year after that? As in advertising research, it is only the significant movement over a period of time that represents any deviation from the norm. An incidental movement can trigger a trend, or it can be just an insignificant blip on your charts. Nor is it the up-and-down popularity of party leadership that counts. It is how such leaders are perceived in relation to the key public issues. That is what you must track. Where is the public moving on taxation, the GST, employment, the environment? Are they more positive or less positive than they were previously? How do they perceive the leadership as far as a particular policy is concerned? That is where you find your strategy: To take them where they want to go within your policies.

Once you have obtained such information, then you have to analyze it to see how it dovetails with the party platform. Which issues should be brought front and centre, and which ones should only be given cursory acknowledgments? How does the leader project on these issues? Devious? Sincere? That is the way you present your party so you can win. Any simplistic approach without a distinct rationale is like shooting dice in the dark. You don't know whether you're winning or losing.

Because of Trudeau's personal magnetism, especially on camera, I was happy when I was producing the free-time political broadcasts, which ranged anywhere from five to twenty

PRIME MINISTER · PREMIER MINISTRE
Ottawa, Ontario
K1A 0A2

September 3, 1984

Dear Jerry:

I apologize for my delay in replying
to your letter of June 19th. Thank you for
your good wishes.

Sincerely,

Jerry Goodis, Esquire,
   Chairman,
      Commonwealth Systems, Inc.,
         45B Hazelton Avenue,
            Toronto, Ontario.
               M5R 2E3

*A letter from **The Right Honourable John Turner***

minutes. He was always more than accommodating because he was astute enough to know where his strengths lay. And television, especially, is a one-to-one medium — you and the individual watching. That is the type of contact he was happy with. It was his style. He especially seemed to enjoy the group discussions in which we lined up people from various walks of life and filmed the spontaneous conversations that developed when he joined them. Because he liked people, he was comfortable; far more comfortable than at a podium or in a media event.

He *did* like them until I organized one group in which I had purposely included a number of NDP supporters. Naturally, I warned him beforehand. I was a little taken aback at his angry reaction. I told him: "So they egg you on, Mister Prime Minister, so you respond and we'll get some good footage." When he finally was persuaded to do it, he handled them beautifully. The anger had ended like a summer squall. But I sure learned that he had a mercurial temperament.

He wasn't a morning person. Once before the 1979 election, I had a photo session arranged for Kensington Market in Toronto. In order to fit it into his tight schedule, we had to do it very early. When he arrived, I could see he was in a foul mood. With a good deal of temerity as we walked along the road to the shoot, I explained that I had arranged for him to visit a chicken dealer and be photographed holding one of the man's products by the neck. It was to accompany a magazine article about his reminiscences of Toronto.

He stopped, glowered at me, and said there was no way he was going to be photographed with any damn chicken. Then he turned and walked away. I was aghast. I had spent days on this assignment, not just setting up the photo, but arranging for the street to be cordoned off, doing a sweep of the area with the RCMP. All those things you have to do whenever the PM descends anywhere.

When I looked across the street, I spied Jim Coutts grinning and shrugging his shoulders. There was no help there, so I took off after the Prime Minister. When I caught up to him, I asked him if he was willing to "blow an election" simply because of a chicken. He stopped, glowered at me again, then walked back to where the poor man (who spent hours bathing the chicken pure white) was standing outside his store, wondering what was going on.

Well, talk about a change in character. The Prime Minister could not have been more charming and friendly. And although he wouldn't actually hold the chicken, we got our photograph. Then he stalked off again — with a parting glower for me — to get back to Ottawa for his Cabinet meeting.

I have great respect for politicians. It doesn't mean I like some of them, even many of them. I respect them because politics is a tough career. You are always in the spotlight. Your personal life can become an open book. It is difficult to maintain your privacy. As well, so many people are after you because you represent them, or because you are supposedly an expert on a specific topic of national or provincial interest. I don't think I could take that consistent pressure.

When we were working on an election campaign, we could get out of Ottawa and return to a normal existence. Politicians cannot. Of course, I wouldn't mind making a couple of speeches in Parliament. But I couldn't stand the constant reminders that someone, somewhere, whom I didn't know, had written me a letter asking for help because they were a constituent. I couldn't stand the constant swing from one issue to another in Parliament and trying to keep up with what was going on. It would be like changing clients every week, then coming up with new campaigns almost as frequently.

But I must admit, I like being involved on my own terms, within my own area of expertise. That's having it both ways, and I love it. Then, too, as Sam Slick said, "Human nature — the best book a man can study after all, and the only true one."

Sam would have made a good politician.

The Right Honourable Pierre E. Trudeau & Jerry Goodis during a Kensington Market tour in Toronto, Ontario — 1978 general election.

CHAPTER
ELEVEN

How Dare the Governments Inform the Electorate!

Question: What is the most difficult and trying task in advertising?

Answer: Producing creative ads for governments, especially the Government of Canada. In my career, agencies with whom I have been involved have handled as much, in total, as one hundred and fifty million dollars worth of government advertising. While that may seem an inordinate amount of money, it really isn't when you consider that, in 1989 alone, the Federal Government spent eighty-nine million by itself. And the provinces about the same collectively. Indeed, Ottawa is the largest advertiser in the country, at least fifteen million dollars ahead of Procter and Gamble.

All sorts of obstacles prevent good government advertising. The first is that most creative people are attuned to thinking in terms of products and services, not legislation or policy. The two creative procedures are worlds apart. With a product you zero in on its obvious, built-in advantages to consumers. With legislation, you must explain the intricacies of legislation or policy in terms people can understand. That means you have to turn copywriters' heads inside out and make them think differently.

The problem is equally one of concept as it is of specific copy. The first must capture what is often not a simple proposal, but a complex issue. The second must explain its intricacies in words that are easily understood, but accurately reflect the intent of the law or policy. And you cannot just choose the easy topics and ignore those that are complicated. To some, that may appear an admission that advertising creative people are shallow. Admittedly, they're not experts in every field of endeavour, yet they may work in any number of areas of commerce and business from banking to frozen foods, from travel to automobiles. With each task, they must analyze the fundamental purposes of the advertising and synthesize what they learn into an image that attracts and explains with as few words as possible.

Despite the intricacies of business, creating government ads is light years removed from what ad people normally do. Some can do it, others cannot. I would think it is closely akin to taking a couple of fashion editors and appointing them to the parliamentary Press Gallery. Their first story out of Ottawa might read: "In introducing legislation on water resources in the House of Commons today, Prime Minister Brian Mulroney was dressed in a double-breasted blue suit with a buttoned-down, striped shirt, and a polka-dot tie by Air Canada." That story lead might be totally accurate, but it would not fulfill the requirements of the story, let alone the needs of the reader.

I have seen copywriters and artists agonize for days over a federal advertising campaign, simply trying to pinpoint and explain the benefits of a single piece of legislation. Every time they make one move, something important gets left out. Then it's back to the drawing board. It can be frustrating because it may be three parts interpretation of legal jargon to five — or more — parts accuracy. That is not easy to accomplish when you only have limited time or space to present your case.

The second obstacle is the fact that Ottawa is often a bureaucratic maze with a lot of people dabbling in the advertising process; some because they sincerely wish to contribute, others because it is such a dramatic departure from their normal routines that they want to play advertising expert. The latter can add substantially to the confusion for the agency. Which advice do you take and which do you dismiss? As well, senior civil servants, because of their areas of responsibility, have far more interest in pushing particular aspects of departmental policy than others. And they are highly persuasive people. That is their job.

Then you have a chain of command all the way up to the minister in charge. Getting approval for your creative output can be tedious and tiresome, especially when many in the chain of command you must deal with have a lot more on their minds than simply advertising. Still the procedure, depending upon with which department you are dealing, must be followed. It can be as difficult as working yourself through a maze.

A number of years ago, I was given the task of producing a television campaign for Canada Day. It was an exciting challenge because it was an opportunity to achieve the best balance possible between a visual impact of pride in our country and a feeling of well-being. That is what Canada Day is supposed to impart to its citizens. What we wanted to accomplish was to do it differently and better than anyone else before us.

Everything went well right through to the deputy-minister level. At storyboard stage, we were told to produce the TV ad and the minister would look at it then. I should have known better, but my enthusiasm for the concept clouded my vision. The production was very expensive since we required not only a significant amount of film footage, but also an orchestra and a choir. The music was in the public domain so we cut costs there. When we finished production, everyone was elated, including the deputy-minister. Finally, it was viewed by the Minister herself. She hated it. She didn't like the music. She didn't like the choir. The commercial was banished into oblivion. I raised holy hell with everybody I could get my hands on, including the Prime Minister's Office. To no avail. The Minister's word was final. We had to start all over again — and with a lot less enthusiasm. And a lot more of your money.

The Minister had absolutely no taste in music. Or, to put it another way, her taste was puerile. She would have banned Bach or Mozart if she had been in power when they lived. She imposed her own standards on the whole of the country, even undermined those of her own staff who were on our side. It was insane, but it happened. I wish someone had told us before that she had a tin ear. I won't name the Minister. You figure it out. (Bloody lawyers!).

Another touchy point with federal advertising is that, when you are creating ads for any federal ministry or agency, you must take into consideration French-English sensitivities. Both must be handled delicately. But it also means approvals are more difficult to obtain, both at the concept level and when you get down to the most minute detail. Personally, I have no problems with it, but it does mean you have to exert more discretion and patience. That can be trying, even when you have two distinct and different agencies producing the two language versions. Each approaches the subject from a different perspective, a different cultural advantage.

Finally, there is the other great sensitivity: the opposition parties in Parliament. It does not matter who is in power. Fear of the opposition can undermine a good creative concept faster than just about anything else. And the problem here is that you are mainly dealing — again — with taste, not content. Therefore, it is easy to criticize. Just look at a number of reviews on a high-profile Hollywood movie. They can range the whole spectrum from "excellent" to "moronic". And there are a lot more opposition critics in the House of Commons than there are movie critics in the country. Once the opposition decides it doesn't like a government ad campaign, then it is fair game for everybody. The news media jump on the bandwagon, often becoming additional critics. And the hype just bubbles up until you wonder why you ever wanted the account in the first place. Is it any wonder then that so much federal government advertising is bland, innocuous, even dumb? Is it a surprise that it is often so safe it's almost sanitized?

If you want a comparison within government departments, look at the ad campaigns for the Department of Tourism in comparison with those of, say, Revenue Canada. The former can be as creative as it wants because it brags about Canada and is mainly seen abroad. The latter must be so delicately handled that you may have difficulty understanding what it is trying to tell you. Sensitivity, sensitivity, sensitivity. It is not an easy task to do good advertising for the feds. It aged all of us involved.

Advocacy advertising is now the catchphrase for all paid campaigns that support a cause or an idea. It has also been called controversial advertising, which, in many circumstances, is a misnomer. Although it is not a totally new phenomenon (many revolutionary ideas in the history of the world have emanated from proclamations nailed up in public), its use in Canada over the past two decades has grown disproportionately, generally supported by significant infusions of money. Just look at the advocacy campaigns that accompanied the free trade debate. And GST. Millions and millions of dollars on both sides.

Although I make no pretension to be a communications theorist — other than about advertising, of course — it does seem to me that the introduction of television news back in the early 1950s unwittingly led to the establishment of advocacy advertising as a powerful tool in any debate on public issues. The TV camera can — and does — dramatically zero in on any event and portray it far more explicitly than was ever possible on radio or in print. Once this happened and came to be understood, it took little time for anyone supporting a cause to figure out, that if you wanted to get maximum impct in the public mind, success depended almost entirely on attracting TV news crews.

The civil rights movement in the United States was probably the first to take full advantage of the new medium. And it did so dramatically and effectively. It soon spread to other protests, and has reached the point now at which if you can gather together even a few supporters, who make enough noise and carry enough placards, you get TV coverage. Naturally, the other media, not wishing to be left behind, began to cover such events more extensively. Today, it is possible to organize a protest — or a news media event — in which the reporters and camera people outnumber the participants.

Many of these protests are mounted against what could be called physically established premises that symbolize whatever you are against. Foreign embassies are, for example, an ideal target if you don't like what a certain country is doing. So are government offices and corporate headquarters. It has gotten to the point where practically any cause demands a visible protest symbol to attack. Meeting in a park and hearing speeches just does not cut it as it did in my father's time.

Advocacy advertising is an answer to such protests because governments and companies can seldom respond in a similar dramatic fashion. Once such advertising became acceptable, it didn't take long for the idea to burgeon into other areas as well; for example, corporate protests against government policy, even protests against what was considered unbalanced coverage in the news media.

Of course, there is a continuing debate about whether advocacy advertising should be allowed at all because it is

CANADA

PRIME MINISTER • PREMIER MINISTRE

Ottawa, K1A 0A2
September 25, 1984

Mr. Jerry Goodis,
The Palace Pier,
Suite 2503,
2045 Lakeshore Boulevard West,
Toronto, Ontario.
M8V 2Z6

Dear Jerry,

Thank you so much for your warm congratulations after the election.

My colleagues and I have been given an overwhelming mandate by the people of Canada and we look forward to the challenge of fulfilling our responsibilities. Your encouragement is much appreciated.

Kindest regards,

Yours sincerely,

Brian Mulroney

A letter from The Right Honourable Brian Mulroney

only those who have money to pay for time and space who can afford it. There are even rules within television networks about such ads. The CBC, for instance, will not accept advertising that it considers to be controversial or opinion broadcasting. CTV and the private stations, under a monitoring group called the Telecaster Committee, are less stringent. Radio and print, on the other hand, seem to have little trouble accepting advocacy ads. (Perhaps that speaks volumes about the perceived impact of advertising by the different media themselves.) The question of whether advocacy advertising should be allowed or not is a perplexing one. I think the CBC acts far too arbitrarily. Its guidelines are too open to individual, bureaucratic interpretation. On the other hand, some critics argue the amount of money you have should not necessarily determine the amount of clout you can bring to bear on a social issue. That, they believe, has the potential of depositing too much power in the hands of too few.

But I think that if you are in an advocacy situation, you should be able to use any legitimate means at your disposal to get your point of view across, as long as it has a solid factual basis. I don't just think you can simply accuse someone of wrongdoing without substantiating your case. You must be able to prove your point logically and coherently, and, if possible, back it up with fact.

One of the most effective advocacy programs was one organized by the petroleum industry in Canada. At the time, 1981, it was being pilloried by everyone from the politicians to the public for the inordinate increases in gasoline prices at the pumps. The newspaper ads developed by the industry and its agency showed a simple, old-fashioned gas pump, one with the glass container on top. The container showed how much money in the price of the container of gas went to various participants in the price structure. The greatest amount by far ended up in government coffers, the smallest to the petroleum producers. That ad caused its own furor, but fewer people blamed producers for the price of gas.

In recent years governments themselves have been involved in advocacy campaigns on issues. Mainly, they are non-controversial, which is why I prefer the term "advocacy" over others. Drugs and alcohol. AIDS. The environment. GST. These are but a few examples. It is an educational process and one that took far too long to develop. Governments, on behalf of the people, have a duty to address social issues that are of concern to the vast majority. They are now beginning to do that. Whether they do it well — and successfully — is something that cannot be determined as yet because we lack experience in tracking their long-haul effects. What I do know is that, creatively, it is a double-edged sword. If it is meek and mild, the audience it is intended for will surely tune out and turn off. It may please the people who are concerned about a particular issue, but that means zilch. It must reach the target audience on its terms in a convincing and direct manner. It must "sell" them. That is a tough assignment, especially when government is involved. The other edge of the sword is that it offers creative teams the opportunity for breakthrough advertising. The issues are sensitive. They demand a response by those you are attempting to reach. They generally demand a change, not only in attitude, but in habit as well. That too is tough to accomplish, but a satisfying challenge.

Obviously, advertising is far from being the sole means of achieving social change. But they can be the trigger that begins the process. That is why such advertising must include backup support. It must prompt those affected to take another step to obtain more information. Then it can begin to help solve the problem.

The most controversial aspect of any government advocacy can be defined simply. Should it have the right to employ advertising to promote policy that has not been passed into law? I believe it has not only the right, but the *responsibility* to do so. Many are going to disagree with me. But I believe that if government does not put its legislative point of view across to the public through promotional material and advertising, a vacuum will exist. The average citizen will not have all of the information he or she needs in order to make an objective judgment on that proposed legislation. Especially is this true when the legislation gives rise to seriously conflicting views, not just to the usual rhetoric of politics and self-interest.

I was — and am — against the current free trade agreement. Yet I had no problem with a Conservative government advertising the merits of such an agreement so that Canadians had a fuller understanding of the theory and hoped-for advantages behind it. As well, I refuse to accept the argument that the public is fully and objectively informed of proposed legislation by means of the news media. In the first place, no introduction of government policy is ever presented in the media without comment from its opponents. That, in itself, provides a bias. The more controversial the policy, the more virulent the immediate protest against it. And it is instant protest that may or may not have any merit or foundation in fact. Yet they accompany each other, not clarifying the issue, but confounding it. Indeed, in newspapers, the proposed policy may be attacked in editorials in the very same issue as it is introduced. The more the issue is joined, the more the news is devoted to those in opposition. That is what we call democratic process. But, during this often lopsided debate, the issue in the public mind may become even more clouded, with reactions based on emotion rather than upon fact.

There are instant experts in almost every situation. (I admit that I have been one of them.) That is because subjectivity plays a major role in ongoing news coverage of any issue. Sometimes it plays too major a role. The so-called experts, sought out by reporters, may have totally biased points of view. Indeed, their views may not even be professional, but personal. As long as it provides a story, who cares? After all, the person does have credentials. Therefore, there is both a perceived and actual imbalance to the debate that must be corrected. Government has every right to defend the policy. And it can do it in any format available to it, whether that be cross-country speeches or advertising, printed material or television debates. The fact that advertising is paid for out of the public purse has no bearing on the argument as long as those expenditures are kept within reasonable limits.

I have been involved as a government communications adviser in a number of highly controversial policy issues. One of the most heated was the patriation of the Constitution under the Liberal government of Pierre Trudeau in 1980. The opposition was screaming at the government. The provinces were screaming. So were many special interest groups.

Under the Canadian Unity Information Office we devised an advertising campaign whose sole purpose was to inform Canadians about the issue and to win them to the government point of view. The government had every right to put across its point of view, the same as any opposition to it has every right to attack it. The issue of the so-called "unity advertising" was raised in Parliament. The thrust of the opposition's argument was twofold. How dare the government advertise a single proposal, not a goverment law or government program? How dare it use public funds to support its own policies?

What was the government supposed to do? Sit back sheepishly and let everyone take potshots at it? Opposing viewpoints often get far greater coverage in the news than does government response. Indeed, the strategy of any opposition to anything is to try to dominate the news. And it succeeds because the media will go to any lengths in order to appear to be fair (and sell newspapers to increase circulation. . .). In doing so, however, it just as often relegates the government to a bystander status, the target rather than the initiator.

The vendetta against patriation advertising culminated, in my mind, with an editorial in *The Globe and Mail* on October 10, 1980. It was entitled: "Call it propaganda." *The Globe* summed up "In a democracy the floor is supposed to be equally open to all debaters. The government presents its case in parliament; the opposition parties examine the government case for flaws and offer alternatives. A majority government is almost always in a position to prevail, but it often alters its proposals to meet reasonable opposition objectives. The ideal is to produce legislation that will serve the country. This exceedingly precarious democratic balance can be completely overthrown if the government uses massive amounts of public funds to sell the public on its proposals. Canada does not need a ministry of propaganda."

Very neatly put in sonorous tones of indisputable theory. If the debate was limited strictly to the "floor" of Parliament, I could agree. But it wasn't. It never has been since the introduction of mass communications. In every public policy dispute, practically anyone who has an opinion can get press coverage. Demonstrations can be organized in which there is little substance revealed other than that the protestors don't like the policy. All this is reported across the country. Radio and television commentators throw in their two cents worth. Newspapers write editorials, choosing sides. *The Globe*'s perspective on how democracy works is a throwback to a time when mass communications just didn't exist. It ignores the power that can be generated now to oppose anything. And that opposition is always far more vocal than that of the supporters of any government policy. If you support the measure you leave it to government to deal with. And whether *The Globe* realized it or not, its editorial was itself "propaganda" with a significant readership that could be influenced. It just didn't have to pay for the editorial space, that's all.

An inherent admission in the editorial was that advertising can sway people: "sell" as *The Globe* put it. That is no more a ministry of propaganda than any editorial page or media commentary is a ministry of private influence over public matters. If advertising has that kind of selling power, the churches and synagogues of the country would be full, and the jails would be empty.

That *Globe* editorial did nothing but convince me that government has a right and a responsibility to inform the people it represents about policies it wishes to adapt for their welfare. And that includes advertising to explain policy and offset criticism of it. At least, in my experience, the government advertising has been far more to the point than most opposing forces. Of necessity, it must be.

Some readers may think that I have avoided a certain important question on government advertising until now, maybe even believe I'm going to ignore it altogether. If that is so, I'm sorry to disappoint them.

I helped the Liberal Party during elections and I received a fair share of government advertising in return. That, according to some, is considered patronage, and they don't like it. The word "patronage" has numerous connotations. If I own a retail store and you buy from me, you are a patron of mine. If you are a regular patron, I will undoubtedly treat you — and others like you — better than casual, off-the-street customers. That is only good business. Regular patrons are vital to your success. No one has any problems with that definition of "patronage." Then there is the definition of the word that says it is "the power or action of distributing governmental or political positions and benefits". That brings on all sorts of negative, sometimes justifiable responses. Just as often it is used as an unjustified derogatory term.

Certainly, it is a known fact that none of us who work on Liberal election advertising are paid for that work. We do it because we are Liberals and want to see our Party in office. It was true, as well, that we were treated well by the party if it did attain power. Don't friends and associates look after one another? After all, we aren't fly-by-night advertising people. We have a reputation in the business, a good client list, and track record. And we didn't get all the government business.

The Right Honourable Pierre Trudeau greeting Jerry Goodis, and in the background The Honourable Marc Lalonde greeting Martin Goldfarb on the occasion of a private dinner in celebration of 20 years of working together with Mr. Trudeau and his advisers — 1988.

Some will say that it's still patronage. What the self-appointed critics do not seem to be able to comprehend is that advertising is a service business. No matter who gets the work, the payments are going to be the same as long as the budgets are consistent. Therefore, if you are a good agency, do good creative work and bill properly, why should you be denied getting government business just because you happen to be a member of the party and have worked for it voluntarily during elections?

I understand that regarding political appointments, some could easily be considered patronage if the person who gets the position doesn't appear to have the requisite qualifications. Then there may be a case for making the accusation, unless the circumstances are special — and explained. The same can be said for the purchase of goods by government. If products are bought at an inflated price by government, that is certainly patronage, even dishonest. The same holds true for inferior products if they are purchased just because the company owners happen to be friends of someone in government.

Government advertising contracts made us money, but we earned every cent of it. We didn't try to give government an inferior product. After all, we had a reputation to maintain in the business. And, whatever we did, we generally got the flack anyway.

Did I become involved in Liberal politics just so I could get government ad contracts? Yes and no. In the first place, I wouldn't have become involved deeply in the Party if I didn't believe in it and mainly what it sought to do. On the other hand, I wanted some of the business and I knew I had a better chance of getting it if I became associated with the Party. At the same time, I know I lost a chance at getting some business accounts simply because I was tagged as a "damn Liberal". Those are the chances you take.

I have done a lot of things to win accounts. I have pressured friends to introduce me to people I wanted to meet because there was a possibility of business there. I have joined organizations, attended events, done all sorts of quite legitimate things in order to get business. Every business person does. So I got myself involved in Liberal politics. If I hated it, I would backtrack as fast as Superman. Or Brian Mulroney.

One thing I have changed my mind on concerns the practice of most governments and governmental departments to employ only Canadian-owned agencies. It was a case of "Buy Canadian" and I used to agree with it. Now I think that the field should be more open to competition.

If you have a Canadian ad agency and, say, a U.S. one vying for the same contract — and their presentations are both excellent — then I believe the home-grown one should get the nod. It's a case of "all things being equal". But, if the American agency can do the job better, then it should get the contract. What we all should be looking for is the best that we can buy. It happens now when governments are buying goods. Why shouldn't it be extended to services such as advertising? In the long run, it will make Canadian companies better — and stronger.

To many that may seem a strange proposition coming from me, an ardent nationalist who still continues to rant and rave about the takeover of Canadian ad agencies by the multinationals. It may even seem stranger considering the number of countries who protect their own businesses in every way they can. I just think, now, that the way the world is evolving, it is self-defeating to be overly protective of businesses. If we're going to survive, then we have to be equal to, if not better than the foreign competition. I also believe it will make us more innovative, aggressive — and successful.

Patronage, in a business sense, is based on doing what you do for your customers in the best way possible. In that way you retain them and grow through the reputation you develop with them. Patronage, based solely on nationalism, is a redundancy unless all factors are equal. Then, and only then, should it come into play. Both ways make us stronger, more competitive, don't you think?

Come on, don't you?

CHAPTER
TWELVE

Don't Shoot Until You See
The Whites of Their Thighs

Now I'm going to get into deep trouble. I want to talk about sexism in advertising. Whatever I say, somebody's going to disagree with me. Violently. In every movement you have zealots. It can be a political movement; it can be religious; it can be sexual. It doesn't matter. The point is the zealots are always going to go too far. In everything. And it is true of the women's movement as it is in any other.

Having said that, I must add that I am against exploitation: the exploitation of women, of blacks, of Jews, of children, of anybody. At the same time, I am for representation, especially in a multiracial country such as Canada. When you depict women — especially attractive women — in advertisements, the picture begins to cloud. What is sexist and what is not? What is pandering to the male? What is not? It is a difficult question; an important one but tricky.

In a recent advertising insert for Christina bathing suits such phrases as "bust enhancer", "bust minimizer", "hip minimizer", and "waist minimizer" dominated the headline and ad copy. There was hardly anything about how good the damn suits were for swimming. The perceived benefit was almost totally devoted to how a woman would look in each style of swimsuit. Is that sexist? It's certainly talking about women in terms of physical allure. The audience is women, but does that make any difference? It certainly does. I don't see anything wrong with it if that is what the majority of women are looking for in a bathing suit. And if men want to ogle the women in the bathing suits in the advertising, that is their problem.

On the other hand, there is a television ad for Cascade

dishwashing detergent. It shows a male bringing out two cooked speckled trout and placing them on a dinner table. The other male in the scene suggests opening a bottle of wine. One of the two females at this obvious dinner party for four picks up the wine glass and makes a comment that it's spotted. Not dirty, mind you, just spotted. And the word "speckled" gets in there too, in case you miss the point. Is that sexist?

As far as I am concerned, it is. It graphically illustrates that the woman is more concerned about what the wine glasses look like than she is appreciative that someone has just cooked a beautiful meal. That belittles women. It says they know nothing about anything but what dish detergent to use. It also has overtones of envy, as if the male were usurping this woman's role as chief cook and wine-glass washer. She has to dump on something he did, to save face. It is sick, but the zealots may miss the innuendo. And I can just visualize the copywriter's thinking. Hey, "speckled" has to do with fish, but also with glasses. Let's join the two together. What a great idea. Horseshoes — and other expletives.

The point of the two anecdotes is that the exploitation of women and sex stereotyping are often in the eye of the beholder. Drawing a line is difficult. If you are after male purchasers for a product, i.e., beer, the temptation is to throw in beautiful, curvaceous women to intimate that is how you are going to attract the opposite sex. Unless you do it tastefully and with respect, you are simply exploiting the female. Not to mention making the male appear to be nothing but a gonad-driven barfly.

If, on the other hand, you want to prove a product is light and portable; i.e., a movie camera, you may show a woman operating it. Because women are generally more diminutive than men, it gets across the point graphically. There is nothing wrong with that. It is the same as showing a male model heaving around something, i.e., an extra-strength garbage bag, to prove that it is sturdy and strong.

My biggest professional encounter with sexism occurred in the early seventies at a time when the feminist movement was beginning to assert itself strongly. Our Montreal office got the Wonderbra account. This was a Canadian company which held down the Number Two position in women's garmentwear. One of our copywriters came up with the line:

"We Care About The Shape You're In." Larry Nadler, who headed the family business, was a risk-taker. He loved the line. So did we. We had it set to music and prepared a television campaign around it. The CBC turned it down, not because of the line, but because we had the audacity to show a woman in a bra. CTV had no such qualms, which proves how arbitrary the world can be. Eventually, the CBC recanted and ran the campaign. I do not to this day know whether it was a change of heart, or the network just missed the revenues.

The result of the campaign — not just in TV, but other media as well — moved Wonderbra into a solid, first-place position in its field. It did not happen overnight, but it did happen. The client was ecstatic and we were understandably just as happy. Then the Nadler family sold out its interests to Consolidated Foods of Chicago. About the same time, the company began receiving missives from some women's groups. The gist of them was: How dare you exploit the shape of women's bodies? How dare you make such obvious reference to it?

We were marketing brassieres. What were we supposed to do? Show a package and then try to explain what was hidden inside? It was ludicrous. Our campaign wasn't dirty, it wasn't even suggestive. It simply showed the product, which was intended for women, on women. Shortly after all this began to happen, we lost the account. We were given no explanation. I suspect it was because Consolidated wanted to move it to its U.S. agency, but they never told us that. What we did notice was that our line quickly disappeared from all advertising. Perhaps that was because the U.S. agency couldn't stand to use a Canadian slogan; or maybe it succumbed to the criticism. Either reason was insufficient to drop an ad campaign that had been truly successful.

At the beginning of the nineties the zealots are still out there, ranting and raving at supposed put-downs of women. And seldom, in my experience, are they right. Just as often, they simply miss the ads that are subtly, truly denigrating to women. You have to be blatant to attract the zealots because their minds are overly small and narrow.

Advertising takes the blame for most sexism, as opposed to many movies and magazines. True, the suggestive movie gets a rating that doesn't allow it to be viewed by minors.

The magazines can be seized at the border or, if they sneak across, have to be placed somewhere out of viewing and reach by children. Yet, paperback novels and rock videos seem to get away with it. There is little or no control over them. But an advertisement in any medium is fair game. Why? Because the zealots know they have a greater chance of winning a victory. Behind that supposedly sexist ad is a company that does a lot of business with the public, and is hyper-sensitive to public opinion.

Many companies which sell their products to a broad cross-section of the public, in my experience, shy away from advertising that could be construed as even slightly risqué. They just do not want to take the chance. That's too bad because sex is beautiful. And, if used tastefully — with perhaps a touch of humour — it can strongly emphasize the point about the product you are promoting.

Companies that are going after the youth market use sex all the time. They don't give a damn about the zealots. T & A sells — to both sexes. (Do I have to explain T & A? I hope not.) Jeans is a perfect example. And the photography is always of exceptional quality. I see nothing wrong with the jean ad that had music backing it in which the lyric was simply — and only: "Bum, bum, bum" to a lilting tune. It's humour. It's fun. It gets the message across.

Then there is the male market, especially that for fashion and grooming. One common approach is to have a female draped over the male because he's wearing the right sweater or suit, or the proper after shave. These ads demean women, depicting them as shallow, mindless creatures attracted to the male for the silliest reasons. It's the symbolism of the macho male, which, according to some creative people, obviously is the only way to attract beautiful women. Not only does it stereotype women, it must shatter the ego of a lot of males, especially if they buy the products and their lives don't change one damned iota. Such ads do a disservice to both sexes.

What, then, do I think of ads for female products that are festooned with female movie stars and models, oozing sex? Shampoos, perfumes, rinses, body lotions. Most of them are amusing. Women look at other women to size them up, just as much as men admire them. If you can sell women's products by using a beautiful spokesperson, why not? And, as a corollary, why not other products? It comes down to a matter of how tastefully it is done.

What I detest more than anything in ads, specifically on television, is the portrayal of the housewife. Her life is shown as supremely fulfilled if she can satisfy her brood. Her greatest kick is to see her face reflected in a newly waxed floor. At wash day she is shown as being little better than an envious fool coveting her neighbor's laundry, which is always whiter and brighter than hers. I become nearly as worked up at the portrayal of the male as couch potato, trying, by every means, to avoid some task around the house. It makes no difference that some dumb product comes along to save him any work. It's demeaning, although men seem to shrug it off more easily than women. Perhaps that is because men may feel more secure in the world than women.

The female has been used and abused ever since advertising began. It is time it ended. And anyone who argues that both sexes are now equally abused misses the point entirely. Since we have only two sexes, we have to use either one or both in advertisements. When we do it, let us do it with taste, humour, and an appreciation of the true attributes of both. If an ad calls for a little sex, that's okay. It's an attribute, too. It exists, and no matter how hard you try, you can't ignore it. But you can ignore those critics who are a throwback to a dull, uninspired, puritan world in which everything about sex was dirty. Advertisers who fear the intimation of sex in their ads lest consumers turn away are similarly out of touch.

Comparison advertising: one product is contrasted directly with another in the same ad in order to convince consumers that the sponsoring company's product is better. I have never liked the idea, although there have been a few good campaigns developed around it. Every time I see an ad that compares one product with another, be it Coke and Pepsi, Energizer versus Duracell, or a Nissan car against a select group of competitors' models, I always get the impression the advertisers are saying to me: "Hey, stupid, we don't think you're smart enough to know the difference between these products, so we are going to tell you." That insults my intelligence.

Take Coke and Pepsi. I don't give a damn if Pepsico carries out a bunch of blind taste tests and comes up with the conclusion that more people like its product. It's a private matter of taste and no one is going to tell me what I should like and what I should not, especially based on the opinions of strangers. They may be cretins for all I know.

In battery comparisons, you generally have little toys — or whatever — churning away until one is still operational. That is the sponsoring company's one. Is anyone really surprised when this fact is finally revealed to us? But, nowhere in the ad does it say how much longer that particular battery lasts. Five seconds? Five minutes or five hours? If it's either of the first two, does anyone care? And unless you know this pertinent fact, all you are dealing with is comparative mumbo-jumbo.

I suppose you could argue the manufacturers of cars have a point because of the large expenditure involved. Comparisons could help when you are putting out, perhaps, twenty thousand dollars or more on a car. My major complaint here is that the sponsoring model is simply pointing out to the prospective purchaser that there are other models similar to it. Therefore, in order to be sure, I should take a look at them before I make a decision. That is poor marketing. The essence of advertising is to point out the benefits and advantages of your product, not to compare benefits and advantages with those of competitors. Leave that to the consumer-advice magazines and the buyer's own intelligence.

Some campaigns in which an intimated comparison has led to the highlighting of a particular product benefit can work. The most famous, of course, was Avis Rent-a-Car. Certainly it was positioning itself against Hertz when it admitted it was Number Two. Then it turned that to its advantage by stating: "We Try Harder." Consumers can understand that. The underdog has to strive more in order to catch the leader in any business. It's a natural, understandable instinct. The only problem with it is that, once Avis used it, it was difficult for other products or services to copy it. A copycat campaign, unless it is done with humour, can turn people off. They do not like the theft of ideas any more than they like the theft of property.

Comparison advertising occurs only between products that are leaders in their field. I then get the distinct feeling the agencies have run out of ideas in either maintaining their position, or taking over the position of the product that's the leader. If that is the case, it would be far better if they simply rethought their advertising strategy. Then they might come up with something new rather than taking the easy — but undignified way — out. Leave comparison shopping where it belongs — with shoppers.

Television can be an insidious medium, especially as it affects small children. Take for example, the marketing of food, drink, and toys. What a child sees on TV, a child wants — automatically.

I have grave concerns about such advertising. In the first place, because of their immaturity, children cannot really discern the difference between the programming and the advertisements. The latter just happen to be shorter. Secondly, the child is not mature enough to decide for itself.

Jerry Goodis as a celebrity clown in the 1989 Toronto Santa Claus parade.

Therefore, you are taking an unfair advantage when you push child-oriented products to pre-schoolers on television. Many of these advertisers — and their agencies — may argue that, since the parents have the final decision in the purchase, the advertising is not harmful. But raising children is a difficult enough proposition without having to battle with them over what cereal or drink or toy you are going to buy for them.

Pre-school children have no idea of what is good or bad for them. Arguing against a commercial that has seductively won a child's interest and desire is an unfair proposition to thrust upon parents, especially if the parents have not even seen it. It forces the parents to needlessly investigate it; then, if they decide the child shouldn't have it, trying to discuss why. As well, children at this age have no idea of what money is. Some of the products may be out of the reach of parents' pocketbooks, especially toys. Others may force a decision between something the child truly needs in his or her growth development against something they do not require, but has become engrained in their minds as necessary.

At this point only Quebec, as far as I know, has banned advertising on television aimed at children under twelve. I think there should be a total ban. Let adults make the decisions on behalf of their offspring, not the children themselves. Too much pressure can be put on them by crafty copywriters.

This leads me into the question of what products should — or should not — be allowed to be advertised and in what media.

Read on.

CHAPTER
THIRTEEN

The Goose and the Gander

The first advertisements for female hygienic products appeared on television in Canada during 1972. Prior to that, such ads, specifically for sanitary napkins, were restricted voluntarily to the glossy women's magazines (the first advertisement in Canada, interestingly enough, appeared in *Maclean's* in 1927).

Understandably, after this product was introduced to TV, the Canadian Radio and Television Commission, responsible for overseeing electronic content in the country, established guidelines to make sure the ads were in good taste. Still, many people were offended, especially women who didn't believe such personal matters should be discussed on TV at all. And the conservative elderly.

At one point, the controversy reached such a level that many daily newspapers devoted lengthy features to it. Some even included protest coupons to try to measure public reaction. Although these elicited a strong negative response, almost two decades later, the ads are still running. And even more of them. From the beginning, the manufacturers of these products countered arguments against the use of TV by pointing out that, in the late sixties and early seventies, there had been numerous revolutionary changes in the design and benefits applicable to female hygienic products. Television was the best way of getting that message across to women — and also potentially increasing each company's share of the market. The companies certainly did not wish to offend women. That would have had the reverse effect of what they wanted to achieve. Therefore, they were as sensitive to the tastefulness of the ads as was the CRTC. And sensitive productions undoubtedly allowed them to prevail.

The initial controversy of advertising sanitary napkins and tampons on television has undoubtedly faded, if it hasn't disappeared completely. That is not surprising, given the fact that the equally sensitive issue of male and female sexuality is now discussed openly and explicitly on radio and television, not to mention government-sponsored TV advertising advocating the use of condoms because of the potential threat from AIDS.

The more important question is whether there really are products and services that should not be advertised. As well, there is the supplementary one of whether there are some that should be restricted with regard to the available media. These questions involve many subtleties.

I have never handled a cigarette account. I've had a number of opportunities to do so, but turned them all down. That doesn't make me a saint. It is just that I personally do not believe tobacco should be promoted through advertising. Of course, it has been banned from television and radio for years. I don't think it should be allowed anywhere, whether it be print, billboards, point-of-purchase displays in stores, or sponsorship of sporting and cultural events. My feelings have been well known for more than two decades. I am not a johnny-come-lately to this issue. During that course of time, I've made innumerable speeches on the subject. At one point, my stance even cost us an account.

Once we had the advertising for Formosa Springs, a small brewery in Ontario. It wasn't a large account, but we enjoyed it. One of the creative lines I liked the most was: "If We Hurried Our Beer, We'd Lose Our Head." Not bad on a small budget. And, for a regional beer, it did well. When Formosa was purchased by Benson & Hedges, one of the tobacco giants in Canada, I was invited to lunch by the president of the takeover company. He told me we could keep the beer account if I stopped making anti-smoking speeches. I declined. Our agency was unceremoniously fired.

My protests against tobacco advertising are so well documented that the Federal Government's Department of National Health and Welfare asked me, in 1989, to act as its advertising expert when a civil suit was brought against it by the tobacco industry. It was an effort to restrain the government from implementing its legislation banning all cigarette advertising in Canada. I was happy to accommodate the Department, even though it came under the aegis of a Conservative government.

In that submission I pointed out that, even though there are nearly two hundred brands of cigarettes available in Canada, the vast majority of them are controlled by only three companies. Although they may appear to be competing against each other for market share, the brands are so similar, they are almost interchangeable. The differences are so small as to be negligible. In almost every brand, there are mild, medium, medium light, light, and extra light; the basic differences essentially being the amount of tar and nicotine they contain.

Why, then, is so much advertising devoted to these products, especially when the number of smokers has been decreasing steadily since the early '80s? Was it an effort to salvage each company's share of a dwindling market? That didn't seem to make much sense, especially since there were so many brands, and the competition was among such a few companies. There had to be another reason.

The true target group in such advertising is not really present smokers. It is to try to convince the impressionable young to take up the habit by any means possible. Most of the advertising is devoted almost exclusively to lifestyle. In a du Maurier print ad, for instance, two young people of indeterminate age are depicted in a four-color photograph. They could be teenagers or they could be in their mid-twenties. They are listening to a high-tech stereo system in a glamorous living room setting. The main line in the ad says: "For people with a taste for something better". Is this ad selling "cigarettes" to mature, upwardly mobile young men and women who already smoke (a relatively small audience, as the statistics bear out), or is it selling "smoking" as being associated with glamour, wealth, and happiness to anyone under thirty (a large audience), which includes a high percentage of adolescents? I suggest it is the latter.

Another ad for Player's Medium stretches credibility, except perhaps to the young. Under a headline that states: "A taste you can call your own", it shows a virile, young male on top of a mountain enjoying a cigarette. He's celebrating his achievement of climbing this peak. Does this mean that Player's Medium is mild enough to allow you to climb mountains? Does it mean that smoking Player's is not injurious to your health? It's male machismo, nothing else, and directed at adolescent males stupid enough to be taken in by it. It certainly didn't take in any actual adult smokers I showed it to. They just laughed at it. A few even commented that it reminded them of the Marlboro man in vintage U.S. cigarette advertising with his brand-image tattoo and rough 'n ready outdoor clothes.

How does such advertising sway young people? Easily. The visceral thrust of all adolescents is to emulate adulthood. They believe that, once they can throw off the shackles of childhood, they'll be on their way to social success, fulfillment, and personal gratification. And most of them can hardly wait to get there, whether they admit it or not.

Lifestyle cigarette advertising caters to these desires. To the guileless and inexperienced young, the cigarette represents a symbolic means of achieving adulthood in a simple, outward manner, before most other advantages of growing up can be attained. And if it is propagated strongly enough, it will succeed with a significant segment of that youthful target audience.

There are other symbols of easily attainable adulthood for adolescents, of course. Alcohol. Drugs. Sex. We, as mature, concerned adults, attempt to protect our young from such potential perils in their formative years. And it is done in every way possible. At home. In our schools. In advertising sponsored either by governments or concerned organizations. To a certain extent, however, we have ignored the cigarette as not being as threatening as the other symbolic activities. It is not perceived as an immediate threat to the young. Venereal or other sexual diseases have an immediacy to them that cigarettes do not. The possibility of pregnancy certainly does for women. Alcohol and drug addiction, after only a short period of time, can be far more devastating a habit than tobacco. The young may realize cigarettes are the leading cause of cancer and heart disease. But that is years hence and, anyway, they figure they can always give them up. After all, it's just a cigarette.

As I concluded in my submission to the Superior Court of Quebec, where the case was being argued: "Based on my advertising experience and knowledge, it is my profound conviction that the tobacco industry is intent on making every effort to systematically and insidiously infiltrate this potentially explosive market (adolescents), and to target it as the only true, large, and profitable one for the future sales of cigarettes, despite which brand may be chosen.

"Present-day tobacco advertising, I grant you, may be subtle, but let me remind the court that, in advertising, we deal with emotional issues, which may be projected subtly, but are conceived to transform our desires into reality. For we are all human, reacting positively or negatively to almost all emotional stimuli. And especially is this true of the young.

"The youth of Canada automatically longs for the lifestyle of the rich, famous, and successful. For the tobacco industry, the cigarette is the symbol of that initial — and available — striving for such a lifestyle. It is truly advocacy advertising through physical and symbolic association. If I developed advertising for the tobacco industry, that is the target market I would strike at. The present creative approach is also the one that I would employ. It is truly seductive advertising. And it is the primary reason why the vehicle of advertising must be denied to the tobacco industry if we are to evolve towards a smoke-free, more healthy society, especially for succeeding generations of our young."

Should other lawfully advertised but potentially injurious products, such as beer, wine, and liquor, be advertised? They, too, are equally symbolic of adulthood to the young. And, indeed, the drawing of such a line is a subtle one. I've handled beer advertising, and the account for a large distillery, Hiram Walker, for many years. What is the difference?

In the first place, no liquor advertising is allowed in Canada on television and radio. Therefore, its promotion is restricted. Secondly, its sale in bulk form in every province is confined to government outlets, which have precise regulations on who may buy it. Although those laws can't always be enforced as strongly as we might want, still they are far more stringent than those concerning cigarettes. After all, if you can buy tobacco in a drug store, can it be all that bad? Finally, the number and kinds of liquors are diverse, and individual tastes are equally distinct. That, in itself, affects the amount of the advertising dollars that can be devoted to each individual brand or product. I believe adolescents are more confused about, and less susceptible to liquor as an easily accessible status symbol than is the example of cigarettes.

What about beer? Most brewery advertising, especially on the electronic media, is almost solely devoted to the youth market. Just look at the lifestyle TV ads associated with its consumption. Although there are distinctions among various product categories — between ale and lager, and between light and dry — beer is essentially beer. It comes in a bottle or a can. It has approximately the same alcoholic content. Why then is it allowed to be advertised?

I suspect it is because the beer lobby, being mainly in the hands of a few large breweries, is more powerful than the distillers in the country. But that is pure speculation. Wine can be advertised anywhere beer can. Does it, like beer, also have a huge, almost monopolistic, grip on the marketplace? Not really. Although certain provinces have substantial wine industries, most wines consumed in Canada are of a foreign vintage. Why, then, can it be allowed a greater capability of advertising than liquor? Again, I have little idea.

Obviously, beer and wine are considered less hazardous by government regulators than liquor. You have to consume more volume to become intoxicated. Yet beer, at least, plays an obvious symbolic role with the young. Some experts in the field say beer is an alcoholic product that is easier to acquire a taste for than either liquor or wine. If that is so, then beer has a better chance of tripping the young than either liquor or wine. If you look closely at the wine ads on TV, you will see they are distinctly different from those for beer. They're mainly associated with social functions or dinners, while beer is almost totally devoted to the singles' scene. If it is not being consumed in bars, then it is at parties or during presumably leisure endeavours. Wine never, at least not in Canada.

We now have liquor and wine being dispensed in coolers. Mainly the ads are devoted to young people having a good time. These products are allowed to be advertised on radio and television. Strangely enough, they are banned on the two media in the United States. Perhaps that is why they have succeeded in making a greater penetration into the markets here than in the U.S.

From all of this you can easily deduce that government often discriminates as to who can advertise different alcoholic products in what media. There seems to be no single guiding principle. Should there be? I believe so; but, as is so often the case, governments have a tendency not to act unless they are pressured into doing so. And a preponderance of that pressure depends upon whether the product or service is seen by most as being "socially acceptable" or not. Cigarettes went out of favour years ago. Beer and wine both have large followings, although generally with distinct groups of people. Liquor is popular, but I suspect its potential from small, concentrated quantities makes it appear more potentially dangerous. All this, of course, is based on supposition. On the other hand, if you look at the advertising regulations, the guidelines they appear to follow also seem based more on supposition than anything else.

Whatever your taste in alcohol consumption, there also lies your prejudice as well as your preference. That prejudice may also cloud your attitudes as to where such products may be advertised. Or even if they can be advertised. Nondrinkers may want all of them banned on all media. Beer drinkers in most provinces ask why they cannot buy their product in a grocery store. Wine and liquor consumers don't seem to give a damn, as long as it is available. Perhaps that is because you can take it home in a single bottle, rather than in a case. To a large extent, we express ourselves on these issues in terms of what we think should be done, depending on what we ourselves do. And, taking it one step forward, what we think should be done is clearly reflected in our attitudes toward the advertising of alcoholic beverages.

A similar duality exists where some other products are concerned too. The Ontario governent, for instance, can promote the use of contraceptives in TV advertising because of the threat of AIDS. Yet contraceptive manufacturers are restricted in the ways they can promote their products. This tells me that we place a greater emphasis on the prevention of social problems than we do in allowing others to choose any medium to promote individual products that may be used in that prevention.

But why do we do it? Because, again, social pressures are at work. In this case they probably should be, but that is my own judgment. Others would disagree, arguing that such advertising would increase the use of condoms overall and that would be beneficial in the prevention of veneral diseases as well as, possibly, AIDs. Indeed my imagination runs rampant when I even begin to think about a condom ad on television. To be explicit about the benefits of a particular brand and to do it tastefully would be a real challenge. The scene in the movie *Skin Deep*, where actor John Ritter wears a fluorescent condom in a darkened bedroom, comes to mind immediately. But, again, some would say that was tastefully — and humorously — handled. Others would consider it tasteless.

What about escort services? Ma Bell accepts their advertising: pages upon pages of them. And daily newspapers have "companion" columns that, if not explicit, can be suggestive. A recent one in the largest-circulation newspaper in Canada, *The Toronto Star*, advertised: Long-haired beauty, female, 23, gentle and captivating, big brown eyes and gorgeous figure wants professional gentleman, 35 + ."

These are all questions that I can't easily resolve. But they are questions we all have to make the attempt to answer.

Maybe in my next book?

CHAPTER
FOURTEEN

The Churches Are Full; The Jails Are Empty

The future. What does it hold for marketing and advertising; just as importantly, for the consumer? Interesting questions, especially as we head toward the year 2000, the millenium. Few are ready to discuss that pivotal point in history right now because it seems so far away. Yet, it is just over the horizon and we should think about it, even plan for it. Undoubtedly, it will have a profound effect on us simply because it is a new threshold, a new starting point.

Certain events always have a prolonged effect on us. Centennial and Expo '67 changed Canada considerably. Among other things, Expo introduced audio-visual techniques that were to have a lasting impact on many industries, including my own. Indeed, we are still refining their innumerable applications. It also introduced Canada to the world, and gave us a pride that lasted almost a decade. Both events captured our imagination and enthusiasm. All things seemed possible. Then, of course, came the October Crisis, followed by the oil shortage, a recession, and exorbitant interest rates to bring us back down to earth. I think it was a holdover from the excitement of 1967 that, to a certain degree, caused my colleagues to forecast so blithely in 1980 what was going to occur during the next decade. I believe also the troubled times we are moving through now made the industry so fractious in its predictions at the beginning of 1990. But the latter group ignored the millenium.

As we approach the year 2000, I think people everywhere will begin to feel optimistic, will start to plan for a better century than the one we have just passed through. Our nature makes us look to the future for better things. It is the same enthusiasm as when you fall in love, start a new job, or begin a holiday. Practically the whole world will be involved.

The news media, the magazines, television — God bless their pointed little 'pencils — will all prepare for the extravaganza. They will be going back over this century, highlighting all the ups and downs, all the victories and the defeats, all the accomplishments; and, as is their practice, all the things we did not accomplish, but should strive to do during the next one hundred years. And, for the first time in the history of humankind, a century of man's progress will have been recorded in photographs and on film.

I believe the millenium will be upbeat, full of enthusiasm and promise. I look forward to it in the comfort of my retirement.

By the time we reach it, though, we'll also be seeing it through different eyes. That is because, technically, we will be far more advanced than we are now. Perhaps we will even have that newspaper delivered to us electronically as was predicted by some ad men at the beginning of the '80s. The world, for certain, will be closer to begin a global village. On January 1, 1992, the European Common Market will officially come into existence. That will mean thirteen countries in Europe, most of which speak different languages, will act economically as if they were one. Will that not change the world, especially when one adds to the equation the changes that have occurred in Eastern Europe? Will it be for the better or the worse as far as Canadians are concerned?

The many things going on in the world call for — even demand — a certain reserve in forecasting. Predictions concerning even a small segment of them require a balanced approach, set against — as they must be — the larger picture of politics, economics, technology, and social pressures. Although it would be foolhardy to predict too far into the future, I do have some things to say. Unlike many other forecasters, what I will try to do is strike a balance between what I think will happen and what I believe must happen.

Marketing and advertising require substantial change if they are going to successfully fulfill their mandates to both clients and consumers in the future. It won't require monumental upheaval, but appraising the art and science of it with clearer eyes and a different perspective. In a 1977 article published in *The Globe and Mail*, I attempted to define advertising as it affected society then. What I said was this:

"Advertising is accused far too often of creating social mores and changing lifestyles. We don't have the power that people ascribe to us. If we did, our churches would be full and our jails would be empty. Advertising only mirrors values and trends in society. It starts very little.

"There will doubtless be a role for advertising in any future free-enterprise, market-oriented economy. As lifestyles evolve and personal and national goals change, advertising too will adapt to new conditions and attitudes."

We're still adapting. The problem is I don't think we're doing it fast enough in many areas. In others, we're being dragged along like a reluctant pup on a leash for the first time. One of the easiest predictions I can make is that more and more producers of goods and services will become intensely aware of how their products and their packaging affect the environment.

Only in the past year or so we have seen a growing number of supermarkets beginning to market environmentally friendly products. We have seen major producers of consumer goods begin to proclaim on packages the fact that their products do not have certain ingredients in them that present a hazard to the environment, e.g., phosphates in detergents. We have seen major fast-food chains roundly condemned for their use of throwaway containers that are considered long-term waste hazards. The result? They're beginning to alter their practices. We have seen boxes spring up in many areas of the country where recyclable containers and products can be deposited.

I have no doubt that this trend will continue. Once consumer thinking begins to shift substantially, it often carries everything before it. Naturally, I expect marketing and advertising to reflect this mounting public change in attitude in order to keep pace, even to capitalize on it. And there are encouraging signs.

Only recently, Labatt's Ontario Breweries began putting messages in its beer cases stating: "You'll notice a change in the way this product is packaged. We are no longer using cardboard partitions in 24-bottle cases . . . in order to reduce waste. It also helps us in controlling our costs. Thanks to you, over 90% of our bottles, and the majority of our cartons are returned to us. Our bottles and cartons already contain a portion of recycled materials, and are themselves recyclable."

That is just one example of making customers aware that corporate concerns are keeping pace with public ones. Expect more of the same from almost every quarter. As Sam Slick once said: "Circumstances alter cases." The circumstances now are that we have become far more environment-conscious. The case should be made that, whenever possible, companies must adapt to these circumstances and alter the ways they produce products and packaging. Those producers who move to change will have a distinct advantage in the marketplace; those who cannot — or will not — will suffer from it. We may even see small notices on consumer-goods packaging that say: "Please place in blue box when empty."

This does not mean that we will be any more of a selective society in that we will relinquish our urge to purchase convenience foods that are prepared outside the home, or to buy ready-made foods that can easily be heated in a microwave, or otherwise prepared quickly. No, we haven't become that much of a conserver society. Present lifestyles don't allow us enough free time to do things the way our grandparents did or, for some, their great-grandparents. There will definitely be a greater emphasis on quick-and-fast in the coming years, but it will be positioned more to health and fitness. Fewer calories, more protein; less cholesterol, more iron; and on and on. Around such items, the type of packaging will matter less because one perceived benefit will hold more sway than the other. If, at the same time, producers can combine both benefits (health and the environment), they will be able to capitalize more.

Until this point, I've been talking mainly about packaged household goods. What about other products that are not strictly consumable items? Here I think we'll see a trend toward greater efficiency, better buyer protection, more support services. It is an area in which I think hotlines are going to play a far more prominent role in the future. As major purchases, such as cars, stereos, or computers become more complex in their operation, the more you will see customer service becoming a key factor in the marketing of such products.

Even now, most of these items, because of the complicated nature of their workings, can only be repaired by the producer. No longer can you simply take something into the local fix-it shop and have it overhauled. There is too much circuitry, too many parts designed specifically for that product. I would even suggest to you that, in a few years, non-company automobile mechanics won't even know how to begin to tune your car or replace a part. Too many car manufacturers are developing models that have their own technology, requiring someone trained to work on it. You may not like that total dependence on one service outlet, but it is a marketing advantage to the car manufacturers. It also puts greater pressure on them to perform on your behalf. A good example is the Audi Card that all owners of that top-of-the-line vehicle receive when they purchase a car. It's a personal guarantee of quality and service anywhere in the world from an Audi-authorized dealer. And the company advertises the benefit strongly. (It was invented by my good friend, Bruno Rubess.)

That is why I see the hotline directly to the company as being a growing trend, combined with a need for better customer service. Only with a combination of the two can the manufacturer provide the required after-sale backup, plus giving customers an outlet for discussing their problems and obtaining advice, not to mention the companies finding out which of their dealers, if any, are falling down on the job.

Customer access is a natural evolution of technology for two reasons: First, you have to know what problems exist out there in the consumer world because it is no longer a simple one. And finding out where the glitches are is the only way you can adapt your operation in order to solve any that do exist. Secondly, you have to tell consumers you are going to back this complicated mechanism. If you appear not to give a damn, then they will simply go somewhere else, regardless of how good your product is. They demand a security blanket whenever they face advanced technology.

Such service also requires the training of people who will be proficient when a customer phones, especially if it is a complaint. If the company representative can only spout the party line, people will become more incensed than when they first phoned. That demands manufacturers have personable, well-trained people to answer complaints and questions.

Future sales may depend on that rep. I think it will happen, and we will all be better off for it. So will the companies who get into it.

On several occasions, I've phoned what essentially was a hotline. A few times it was to complain. Mainly it was to request more information about special functions or additional features for purchases I had made. In a number of cases, once my query had been answered or my problem resolved, I was asked some simple questions about myself and my purchase. That is market research combined with customer service. Expect to see, and hear, more of it. It could be vital to future marketing.

Customer service is going to be the major trend in retailing. A personal example:

A few months ago my wife purchased an item of clothing at Bretton's in Toronto's Bay-Bloor shopping area. Within days, she received a postcard from her sales clerk asking whether the product — and the service — was satisfactory. That impressed her because she had never run across it before. It also convinced her this was a store to continue doing business with. It was going out of its way to make sure she was a satisfied customer.

A little thing? Perhaps. I was intrigued enough that I investigated the company further. Bretton's is an offshoot of a Dutch-owned company that is one of the world's largest retail establishments. I found what I think the trend of the future in retailing will be.

First, the staff is particularly well trained. The course each employee must go through before meeting the public is intense and thorough. Employees work on an incentive bonus plan, which includes, not only sales records, but such things as prompt arrival for work and proper dress code. Everyone is kept up to date on news involving the company. And, a relationship is individually maintained. This is an example of the way consumers wish to be treated. Future marketing will be based on it; engaging customers, servicing, and retaining them.

I can think of no better marketing plan than that of the FTD florist service. Although it has been around a long time, it is still one of the great marketing ideas of the twentieth century. The fact that you can phone a florist in one city, place an order for someone in another country, and have that order filled within hours is a true marketing benefit. When the service began in 1910, obviously it wasn't as fast as it is now. But look at the advantages to the individual retail florists over all those years, many of whom are independents. Not to mention the benefits to customers.

Naturally, technology has played an enormous role in improving such customer services. It will continue to do so at an even more accelerated pace. We now have fax systems that can deliver hard copies of orders, contracts, and similar required communiqués with, virtually, the speed of light. Because of improved computer systems, some jewellery stores can give you an identification number on any piece purchased above a certain price. What the number allows you to do is get you an updated appraisal on the jewellery in case of loss, theft, or for estate reasons. All you have to do is phone or write, give the number, and get the answer. It is not as fast as fax, but it sure provides a customer benefit for shopping at a particular store. Such a service may only be in Europe, but it is bound to cross borders and continents soon. There is even a system being developed now that will allow customers to have precious stones fingerprinted by laser. Yet another consumer benefit. You pay for such a service, but I think most people now want it. In the future they'll demand it. It is called 'Gemprint'.

Such will be the future of retailing. It used to be that retailers required their staffs to offer "prompt, courteous, efficient" service. It will still be a prerequisite, but will be enhanced and augmented substantially. The three historic retailing guidelines are changing to three new cornerstones, expressed in terms of the consumer, not the staff. They are: "You, the customer, are important, wanted, and welcome." The difference may appear subtle; but it can make the world of difference in business today — and tomorrow.

Retail corporations are finding out quickly that success in business is based on pleasing customers. Quality can be found in many establishments. So can price. In order to retain customers, however, retailers must offer more in both tangible and intangible benefits that will win and hold consumers. Nor do companies simply respond to a board of directors, but to the purchasers of their products and services. That is why you see more corporate presidents in advertisements now. What they are trying to tell you is that they care about you, and that if you are unhappy, then you should let them know. One of the main reasons the pressure is being placed on retailers these days is direct marketing. It is growing so fast in so many product ranges that it is becoming a threatening alternative to normal retail shopping. Where it is going to go in the future is, really, anyone's guess. But, every ounce of technological know-how will be investigated by the industry in order to reach consumers better, faster, and with a greater variety of goods and service.

Anyone with a computer can purchase a modem that allows them to use the telephone to tap into resource centres for information. What the computer owner gets, either simply with the payment of a telephone long-distance charge or a specified fee plus time charges, is a list of printed material from the source. It could be a newspaper listing of articles under specific topic headings, a government resource of available material, or a special service catering to certain needs. When computer customers find what they are looking for, all they have to do is turn on the at-home printer, punch selected keys, and that information is transcribed to them. Let us take it one step further. The more households which have computers — and modems, which are relatively inexpensive — the more direct marketing will have to look at them as a target for their merchandise. What will that mean?

As a computer owner, you may get a portfolio in the mail, listing more than, say, one hundred buying guides that you can tap into with your modem. You can look at what is available, then print out the information you need on what you might want to buy. We are speaking hypothetically. But why not? The technology is in place, the marketing opportunities are there too. All that is needed is enough people with computers — and that is growing daily. It has far greater potential than the cable-TV shopping channel.

One problem in direct marketing is that it is somewhat restricted in what it merchandises. After all, you wouldn't buy an automobile or some other product as complex through the mail or over the phone. There is too much personal preference involved, too many questions to ask. Nor would you buy a suit, or a pair of skiis. Such items have to be fitted to your own personal needs. But even the manufacturers of many such products are looking at ways they can reach consumers in the quiet of their own homes, without the hustle and noise of a showroom floor or a crowded store. That is where the possible incentive to buy, and to buy a particular brand or model, originates.

In the end, it will mean better quality merchandise because the producers will have to be able to tell you more about what they are trying to sell you than they can in a thirty-second commercial. There will be no interference from a salesperson until you actually narrow your decision down to a select few. That, in turn, will mean sales people will have to be more attuned to what the customer already knows and — how that salesperson can close the sale.

What is happening — and will be occurring more in the future — is that the marketing media will be battling to prove that they are both efficient and effective. It will mean that producers will look for a niche in the marketplace for their products and a way of reaching those potential customers with the same effectiveness and efficiency.

Competition has always been good for the consumer. It has also been good for those who design and manufacture goods, as long as they know who their audience is and attempt to reach it with messages that are pertinent to its needs. It is survival of the fittest and involves everyone from the workers to the top executive, from the salespeople to the marketing strategists.

As Sam Slick would have said: "Things can't and won't remain long as they are." I agree with him wholeheartedly.

CHAPTER FIFTEEN

Beware The Eagle's Talons

As advertising in the coming years capitalizes on marketing advantages, it will also have its own row to hoe. Amid the contractions caused by agency mergers and client demands for a more effective use of budgets, are openings for the adventurous and brave-hearted.

There is also a lot of crass creativity around; stereotyped ads featuring lifestyle clichés, silly puns, and inane humour. That means the opportunities for a mini-rebellion on the creative side of the business are open to anyone with a good sense of planning and a fertile imagination. Indeed, I detect signs that it may have begun already. Still, they are mainly only tiny glimmering in the dark.

There is a movement, for example, to employ more down-to-earth actors and actresses in radio and TV commercials. They are more like real people. They can carry on a dialogue that not only makes convincing sense but is delivered in a non-theatrical, personable tone of voice. "You never have a second chance to make a first impression," the key line in a Head & Shoulders shampoo commercial comes easily to mind. The dialogue is between a brother and a sister. It's natural and light, yet competitive; what one might expect in such a situation. That makes it enjoyable to watch any number of times without becoming bored. The argument the girl puts forth is a common-sense one. That makes it all the more convincing. It is simply good advertising for a product that has been around a long time. Perhaps its main tag-line should become the slogan of all creative people in the '90s. With so much competition for the consumer dollar out there, you really may not have a second chance to make a first impression.

There also appears to be more of a trend to using children as foils in advertising directed to adults. They end up being the "smart" ones, proving a point to their elders. When done well, without the children appearing too clever or cute to be believed, it works. Everyone relates to the innocent, straightforward common sense of children. It could also be overdone, which is what often happens when advertising begins a new trend that creates a wave of imitators.

I believe creativity has to get back to reality. That is the first thing. To hell with glitz and glamour. The same goes for lifestyle that is generally way beyond the average consumer's imagination or pocketbook. It is comparable to building nothing but "monster" houses with an endless number of rooms and three-car garages simply because you're going to make a bigger buck than if you are selling a comfortable, three-bedroom home that people can afford to buy — and want. Land is expensive in most major cities, but there must be more imaginative ways of developing it than putting huge boxes on it, or high-rise cells. The same can be said, to a certain extent, for advertising rates in most media. But it doesn't mean you have to spend a fortune on ad production just to show you are keeping up with the rise in media rates. Nor does it mean that you have to allocate most of your budget to the more expensive media just to get impact. That is fiftieth-floor mega-agency snobbism.

The product or service, is what you are advertising. It is what counts, not the kick the creative team gets out of spending as much money as possible to get across a simple message to consumers. And the message is what sells. It must be clear, concise, credible, convincing, and consistent. That's five "Cs" in a row, but it is the only way I can think of to get my message across memorably. If any agency produces an advertising campaign on behalf of a client that doesn't have those five "Cs" in it, then they are cheating that client. If they produce advertising that goes beyond them, then the creative approach is inane. Or illegal.

The problem in many creative departments is that they only want to work on extravaganzas, involving as large a production as the budget — or the client — will allow. Television has done that to them, because that is where the so-called glamour is. If they want to do that kind of thing, let them go into producing rock videos where impression, not content, is the only rule.

I think we are beginning to see a shift in thinking, and enough clients who are beginning to realize that they have been had for too long on the principle that "the bigger the buck spent, the bigger the bang you get." Or, as Sam would put it to certain creative people: "Many a feller looks fat, who is only swelled."

I look for more down-to-earth creativity in the '90s, and expect to see the five "Cs" begin to dominate the concepts that are placed before clients. Much closer attention will be paid to what media should be used to reach a target audience. It will take some rethinking, perhaps even retraining, of creative people. The medium may be direct mail or promotion, print or outdoor, radio or television. It shouldn't matter to the creative staff because each presents its own style and own environment, which, in turn, offers its own opportunities. A new breed of copywriters and artists will look upon each and every challenge as an opportunity to express themselves well in any medium.

Consumers are now more concerned about how they spend their hard-earned money. They know they work almost five months of each year just to pay their taxes, both direct and indirect. Creative people have to appreciate these facts of life. They have to deal with them. That is why I believe there must be a new back-to-basics philosophy in creativity. Inklings of it exist at present, but it must become far more pervasive if people are going to stop flipping pages of advertising, switching stations on their radios, and zapping TV commercials.

I am certain we are going to see more of advocacy advertising in the future. Some of it will be controversial because it will be battling governments, corporations, or special-interest groups. Some, however, will be equally controversial simply because it will take on touchy subjects and talk about them in new creative ways.

Advertising on the topic of substance abuse or person abuse in down-to-earth terms is not what many of us wish to see or hear. Yet that may be the only way to get through to the population generally as well as to specified target groups. Some may argue that there is already enough being written and talked about on these topics. Why then does anyone need advertising as well? Advertising's purpose is not the same as that of news articles or feature programming.

The latter is done to inform. If you do not, however, wish to be informed, you can ignore them easily. Advertising is meant to highlight an issue, to trigger thought and emotion. It is far more difficult to avoid because it comes at you when you least expect it. That is why I see so much potential for advocacy advertising on social issues. It won't solve the problems, but it can make damn sure people understand there are some. It can ram home the fact that help can be obtained to overcome the obstacles to resolving a particular social or political dilemma.

Everyone has a responsibility to society. If we are going to allow the corporate world to spend money defending itself, then we have every right to ask it to help solve broader issues. Companies will be reluctant to get involved. I think they must: with rights come obligations. If you do not fulfill your obligations, then it is conceivable you could have your rights taken away from you. Companies involved in the sale of alcoholic beverages do attempt to fulfill their responsibilities of trying to convince people not to drink and drive. That is commendable. But other sectors should become involved in issues not directly related to their products or services. McDonald House is a perfect example. George Cohon, the top dog at McDonald's, has a heart as big as his ego — and that, dear reader, is *big*. But he has a social conscience even bigger. McDonald House is a way-station for parents from out of town visiting their hospitalized children. It is a marvellous idea, beautifully executed — and George has the good sense not to boast or in any way publicly capitalize on the institution's good work. That is corporate responsibility, and not just involving advertising, but social activism.

All of us live in communities. We have a stake, whether as individuals, retailers, or producers of goods and services. We must become involved in helping resolve the community's problems, especially when we have the wherewithal to contribute significantly. One of those ways is through advocacy advertising which can have an impact on how our community joins together to fight against what attempts to destroy us. For too long corporations have simply tried to throw charitable contributions at the problems. They must take a more active role, even if it is only in their own self-interest. And I think we will see it.

Leading the charge toward a new era in advertising as a

business will be the agencies and boutiques that base their reputations on results, not on pie-in-the-sky promises. That, in itself, should be part of the down-to-earth approach. Some agencies are starting to develop fee relationships with clients based on annual-sales success. In order to strike such a bargain, the agency or boutique must be confident of its own talents. Certainly there will be upturns and downturns as a result of changing economic conditions, but these can be taken into consideration if both the agency and client work them out to each side's mutual agreement. This could result in greater trust, more mutual respect, and a closer partnership in advertising products and services.

In recent years, the single, all-encompassing advertising campaign has come more to the fore. A budget is struck, a campaign developed, and both agency and client go with it. Mainly it was forced on the agencies in order to counteract the escalating costs of production. Unfortunately, it may continue for the very same reasons that bred it. However, it is not the true answer to budget limitations. There is an alternative route, but it requires more imaginative ways of looking at advertising. Why, for instance, does every ad have to look or sound the same? Why cannot variations on the same theme be done to give the creative element a different look, a new twist? What it means is taking a creative concept and playing with it in the same way as one can develop new and interesting menus around the same basic foods.

A recent innovation in the world of graphic arts is called CAD, computer-aided design. Using a special type of computer, graphic artists can now play with the design of, say, packaging right on the screen to the very simulated size the package will end up being. They can switch colour combinations, move components around, highlight certain features, change typefaces, so all the variations can be studied before a final draught is done. Clients can even sit there and watch it happen right before their eyes, making minor decisions which complement the whole.

Agencies could do much the same thing, although not necessarily employing the same technology. To a certain extent it is happening. Some piggyback campaigns on television are a prime example. Two distinct fifteen-second commercials are joined together to form one thirty-second spot, but they can also be broken apart and used separately. There are also both radio and TV commercials that have been edited down from their original size so that a variation on the original version can be aired. Such techniques should be applied more often to more media. Granted it requires imagination and skill, but that is what the client is paying for. That is the way budgets can be used to extend their impact and their reasonable longevity.

The single-ad campaign, repeated ad nauseam, is like being pricked lightly with a pin fifty or a hundred times. After the first twenty or so, one becomes so accustomed to it that you ignore it. The same is true of the same ad on a seemingly endless run. It has no long-term impact. It is a waste of money.

In Canada, because of our two official languages, any advertiser wishing to reach both French and English audiences must produce ads in both. Once the English ads were simply translated into French. That proved to be disastrous. The subtleties of the two languages are as distinct as the words are. The visual images do not always correspond. Hence, agencies began to produce separate versions for each language. Why can't we be imaginative and productive enough to develop single-theme campaigns that have multiple variations built into them? In the long run, it would be to our advantage because, if we do, improvements in technology would be developed quickly to aid us. Necessity may be the mother of invention (Sam Slick, by the way, didn't say that), but innovation is the offspring of challenge.

I was against free trade with the U.S. from the beginning, mainly because I thought it infringed on the growth of the Canadian advertising industry, even threatened it. In a contributory chapter to a book (published by McClelland & Stewart) advocating that such a deal not be entered into, I summed up my views this way under the title: "Beware the Eagle's Talons."

"The eagle in flight is a beautiful sight, a soaring symbol of freedom. But when its shadow swoops across the meadow, small creatures know to scurry to their burrows. They realize that the eagle's talons are sharp and that its beak rips and devours.

"In the marketplace, freedom is a concept we view with healthy suspicion. We flip over the 'free' tag to find the hidden costs. Only the naive believe that anything is truly free.

We would be naive indeed to accept that the so-called free-trade deal with the United States is any different. The agreement our government is trying to get us to accept could destroy our industry, and that is a pretty expensive bargain.

"Too much of what goes on in the Canadian advertising business is already determined in — no, dictated from — the boardrooms of London, New York, Chicago, and Battle Creek. I've sat in those boardrooms and seethed inside as the American executives told me that they had decided as a matter of efficiency to have a U.S. agency, with a branch plant in Canada, handle all of North America.

"I've tried explaining with sickening frequency that Canada is a distinct market, requiring sensitivity to issues of history, language, religion, and culture, and wasted my breath doing it. Our country is no more than an insignificant blip on the sales charts of some of the multinationals. What plays in Dubuque will play just as well in Antigonish.

"I'm not saying Americans are devils. I'm not saying that I don't want to be a friendly neighbour to some of the most vital and interesting people in the world. I like Americans, but I know for sure I am not one, and I want to keep on enjoying the differences between us as well as the similarities.

"That our differences are so subtle makes protecting them that much more important, and difficult. The Americans, for all their reasoning words, are in the marketplace to compete and win. To do this, they will plunder our profession and not be satisfied until the territory is indisputably theirs."

That was a year or so ago. At present, only four of the top twenty-five English-speaking advertising agencies in our country are Canadian-owned. I think it's time we started fighting back, and I hope this book will be a help for those who wish to begin doing it.

One more dance with Sam Slick. He summed it all up neatly, "Support what is right, oppose what is wrong. What you think, speak. Try to satisfy yourself, and not others. And if you are not popular, you will at least be respected; popularity lasts but a day, respect will descend as a heritage to your children."

Well said, Sam. And thank you from a proud fellow Canadian.

PRINTED & BOUND IN USA BY
R.R. DONNELLEY & SONS COMPANY